POKéMON™

LEGENDARY AND MYTHICAL

GUIDEBOOK

DELUXE UPDATED EDITION

Pokémon™

LEGENDARY AND MYTHICAL GUIDEBOOK

DELUXE UPDATED EDITION

SCHOLASTIC INC.

ISBN 978-93-5954-196-9

This reprint edition: June 2025

Interior design by Kay Petronio
Cover design by Cheung Tai

Printed in India at MicroPrints India, New Delhi

CONTENTS

MEET THE LEGENDARY AND MYTHICAL POKÉMON!

The incredible Legendary and Mythical Pokémon you'll discover in this book are straight out of the pages of Pokémon legends. These Pokémon are rare, but they roam every known region of the Pokémon world, from Kanto to Paldea.

Legendary and Mythical Pokémon are incredibly strong, far beyond many other very skilled Pokémon—and that is why they have had so much influence. They are Pokémon who have used their power to shape history, and in some cases, the world.

Turn the page to see everything you'll learn about these amazing Pokémon!

HOW TO USE THIS BOOK

This book provides the basic stats and facts you need to know about every currently known Legendary and Mythical Pokémon. Here's what you'll discover about each Pokémon:

NUMBER: National Pokédex Number

DESCRIPTION: Knowledge is power. Pokémon Trainers have to know their stuff. Find out everything you need to know about your Pokémon here.

NAME

TYPE: Each Pokémon has a type, and some even have two. (Pokémon with two types are called dual-type Pokémon.) Every Pokémon type comes with advantages and disadvantages.

CATEGORY: All Pokémon belong to a certain category.

HOW TO SAY IT: When it comes to Pokémon pronunciation, it's easy to get tongue-tied! There are many Pokémon with unusual names, so we'll help you sound them out. Soon you'll be saying Pokémon names so perfectly, you'll sound like a professor.

HEIGHT AND WEIGHT: How does each Pokémon measure up? Find out by checking its height and weight stats. And remember, good things come in all shapes and sizes. It's up to every Trainer to work with their Pokémon and play up its strengths.

GENDER: Most Pokémon are both male (♂) and female (♀), but some are exclusively one gender or have an unknown gender.

ABILITIES: Most Pokémon have one Ability that can help them in battle. A Pokémon's Ability usually relates back to its type in one way or another. Some Pokémon have one of two possible Abilities.

WEAKNESSES: In a battle, the effectiveness of a Pokémon's moves depends on the type of its opponent. A Pokémon's weaknesses show what other Pokémon types will most successfully be able to damage it in an attack!

EVOLUTION: If your Pokémon has an evolved form or pre-evolved form, we'll show you its place in the chain and how it evolves.

MYTHICAL POKÉMON

#0151

When viewed through a microscope, this Pokémon's short, fine, delicate hair can be seen.

MEW

NEW SPECIES POKÉMON

How to Say It: MUE

Imperial Height: 1'04"

Imperial Weight: 8.8 lbs.

Metric Height: 0.4 m

Metric Weight: 4.0 kg

Type: Psychic

Gender: Unknown

Abilities: Synchronize

Weaknesses: Bug, Ghost, Dark

DOES NOT EVOLVE

76

STATS AND FACTS
ABOUT LEGENDARY AND MYTHICAL POKÉMON

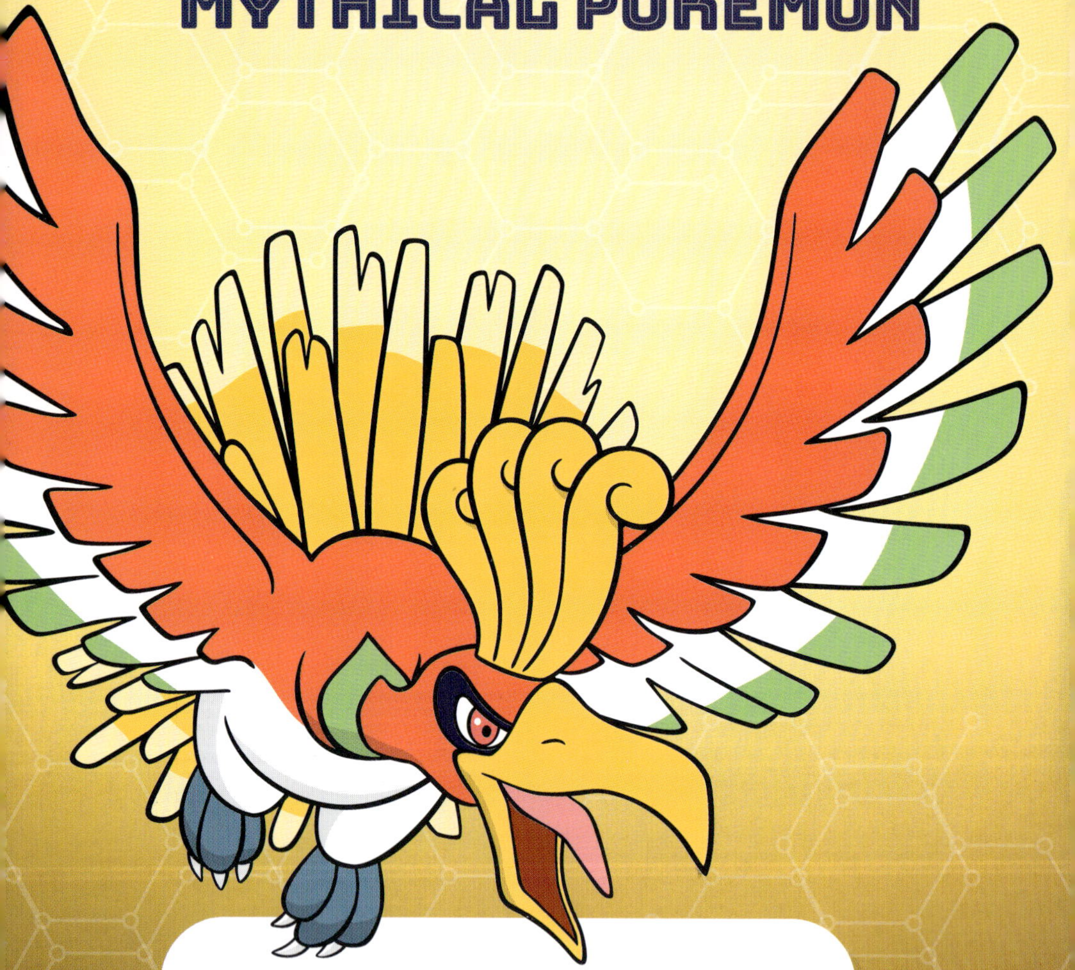

Read on for the scoop on every currently known Legendary and Mythical Pokémon, listed here from A to Z!

#0493

According to the legends of Sinnoh, this Pokémon emerged from an egg and shaped all there is in this world.

It is told in mythology that this Pokémon was born before the universe even existed.

ARCEUS

ALPHA POKÉMON
How to Say It: ARK-ee-us
Imperial Height: 10'06"
Imperial Weight: 705.5 lbs.
Metric Height: 3.2 m
Metric Weight: 320.0 kg

Type: Normal
Gender: Unknown
Abilities: Multitype
Weaknesses: Fighting

DOES NOT EVOLVE

#0144

This legendary bird Pokémon can create blizzards by freezing moisture in the air.

ARTICUNO

FREEZE POKÉMON
How to Say It: ART-tick-COO-no
Imperial Height: 5'07"
Imperial Weight: 122.1 lbs.
Metric Height: 1.7 m
Metric Weight: 55.4 kg

Type: Ice-Flying
Gender: Unknown
Abilities: Pressure
Weaknesses: Steel, Fire, Electric, Rock

DOES NOT EVOLVE

#0144

Its feather-like blades are composed of psychic energy and can shear through thick iron sheets as if they were paper.

Known as Articuno, this Pokémon fires beams that can immobilize opponents as if they had been frozen solid.

GALARIAN ARTICUNO

CRUEL POKÉMON
How to Say It: ART-tick-COO-no
Imperial Height: 5'07"
Imperial Weight: 112.2 lbs.
Metric Height: 1.7 m
Metric Weight: 50.9 kg

Type: Psychic-Flying
Gender: Unknown
Abilities: Competitive
Weaknesses: Ghost, Dark, Electric, Ice, Rock

DOES NOT EVOLVE

#0482

Known as "The Being of Willpower." It sleeps at the bottom of a lake to keep the world in balance.

It is thought that Uxie, Mesprit, and Azelf all came from the same egg.

AZELF

WILLPOWER POKÉMON
How to Say It: AZ-zelf
Imperial Height: 1'00"
Imperial Weight: 0.7 lbs.
Metric Height: 0.3 m
Metric Weight: 0.3 kg

Type: Psychic
Gender: Unknown
Abilities: Levitate
Weaknesses: Bug, Ghost, Dark

DOES NOT EVOLVE

#0898

Calyrex is a merciful Pokémon, capable of providing healing and blessings. It reigned over the Galar region in times of yore.

Calyrex is known in legend as a king that ruled over Galar in ancient times. It has the power to cause hearts to mend and plants to spring forth.

CALYREX

KING POKÉMON
How to Say It: KAL-ih-reks
Imperial Height: 3'07"
Imperial Weight: 17.0 lbs.
Metric Height: 1.1 m
Metric Weight: 7.7 kg

Type: Psychic-Grass
Gender: Unknown
Abilities: Unnerve
Weaknesses: Fire, Ice, Poison, Flying, Bug, Ghost, Dark

DOES NOT EVOLVE

Turn the page to see more forms of Calyrex!

#0898

According to lore, this Pokémon showed no mercy to those who got in its way, yet it would heal its opponents' wounds after battle.

It's said that this Pokémon once moved a large forest—and all the Pokémon living there—to a new location overnight.

ICE RIDER

CALYREX

HIGH KING POKÉMON
How to Say It: KAL-ih-reks
Imperial Height: 7'10"
Imperial Weight: 1,783.8 lbs.
Metric Height: 2.4 m
Metric Weight: 809.1 kg

Type: Psychic-Ice
Gender: Unknown
Abilities: As One
Weaknesses: Fire, Bug, Rock, Ghost, Dark, Steel

DOES NOT EVOLVE

#0898

It's said that Calyrex and a Pokémon that had bonded with it ran all across the Galar region to bring green to the wastelands.

Legend says that by using its power to see all events from past to future, this Pokémon saved the creatures of a forest from a meteorite strike.

SHADOW RIDER CALYREX

HIGH KING POKÉMON
How to Say It: KAL-ih-reks
Imperial Height: 7'10"
Imperial Weight: 118.2 lbs.
Metric Height: 2.4 m
Metric Weight: 53.6 kg

Type: Psychic-Ghost
Gender: Unknown
Abilities: As One
Weaknesses: Ghost, Dark

DOES NOT EVOLVE

#0251

This Pokémon came from the future by crossing over time. It is thought that so long as Celebi appears, a bright and shining future awaits us.

CELEBI

TIME TRAVEL POKÉMON
How to Say It: SEL-ih-bee
Imperial Height: 2'00"
Imperial Weight: 11.0 lbs.
Metric Height: 0.6 m
Metric Weight: 5.0 kg

Type: Psychic-Grass
Gender: Unknown
Abilities: Natural Cure
Weaknesses: Fire, Ice, Flying, Poison, Bug, Ghost, Dark

DOES NOT EVOLVE

#1004

It controls flames burning at over 5,400 degrees Fahrenheit. It casually swims through the sea of lava it creates by melting rock and sand.

The envy accumulated within curved beads that sparked multiple conflicts has clad itself in fire and become a Pokémon.

CHI-YU

RUINOUS POKÉMON
How to Say It: CHEE-yoo
Imperial Height: 1'04"
Imperial Weight: 10.8 lbs.
Metric Height: 0.4 m
Metric Weight: 4.9 kg

Type: Dark-Fire
Gender: Unknown
Abilities: Beads of Ruin
Weaknesses: Water, Ground, Fighting, Rock

DOES NOT EVOLVE

#1002

This Pokémon can control 100 tons of fallen snow. It plays around innocently by leaping in and out of avalanches it has caused.

The hatred of those who perished by the sword long ago has clad itself in snow and become a Pokémon.

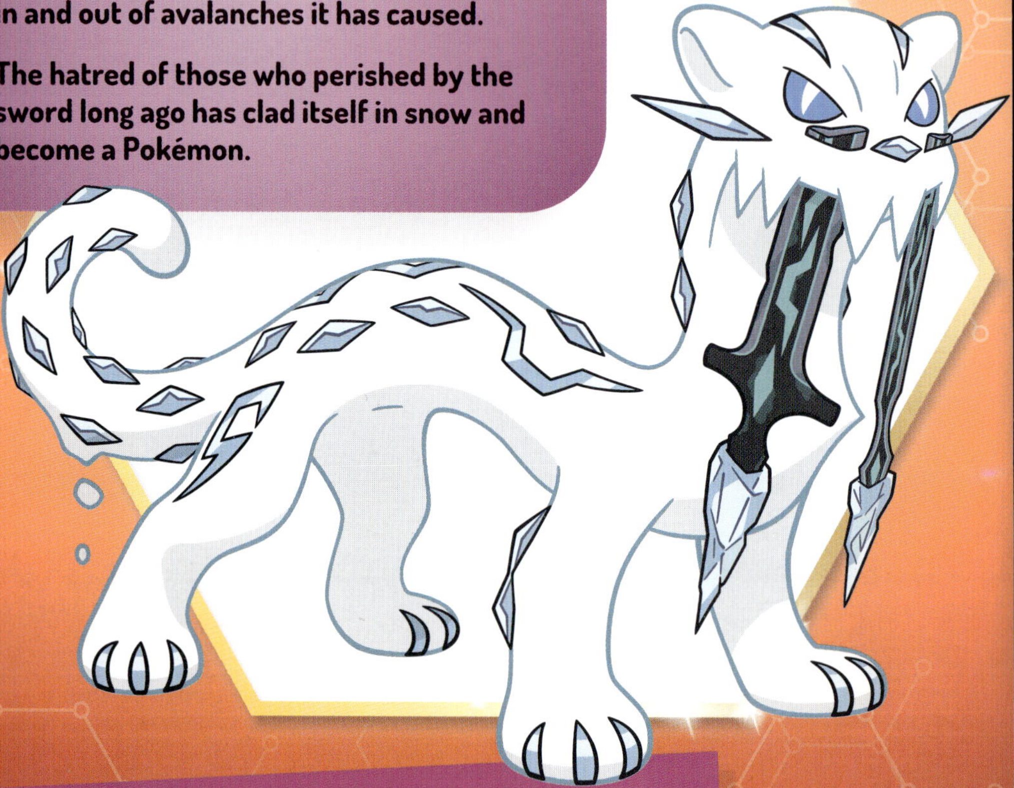

CHIEN-PAO

RUINOUS POKÉMON
How to Say It: CHYEHN-pow
Imperial Height: 6'03"
Imperial Weight: 335.5 lbs.
Metric Height: 1.9 m
Metric Weight: 152.2 kg

Type: Dark-Ice
Gender: Unknown
Abilities: Sword of Ruin
Weaknesses: Steel, Fire, Fighting, Rock, Fairy, Bug

DOES NOT EVOLVE

#0638

This Pokémon appears in a legend alongside Terrakion and Virizion, fighting against humans in defense of the Unova region's Pokémon.

From the moment it's born, this Pokémon radiates the air of a leader. Its presence will calm even vicious foes.

COBALION

IRON WILL POKÉMON
How to Say It: koh-BAY-lee-un
Imperial Height: 6'11"
Imperial Weight: 551.2 lbs.
Metric Height: 2.1 m
Metric Weight: 250.0 kg

Type: Steel-Fighting
Gender: Unknown
Abilities: Justified
Weaknesses: Fire, Fighting, Ground

DOES NOT EVOLVE

#0790

The king who ruled Alola in times of antiquity called it the "cocoon of the stars" and built an altar to worship it.

As it absorbs light, Cosmoem continues to grow. Its golden shell is surprisingly solid.

COSMOEM

PROTOSTAR POKÉMON
How to Say It: KOZ-mo-em
Imperial Height: 0'04"
Imperial Weight: 2,204.4 lbs.
Metric Height: 0.1 m
Metric Weight: 999.9 kg

Type: Psychic
Gender: Unknown
Abilities: Sturdy
Weaknesses: Bug, Ghost, Dark

#0789

Even though its helpless, gaseous body can be blown away by the slightest breeze, it doesn't seem to care.

Whether or not it's a Pokémon from this world is a mystery. When it's in a jam, it warps away to a safe place to hide.

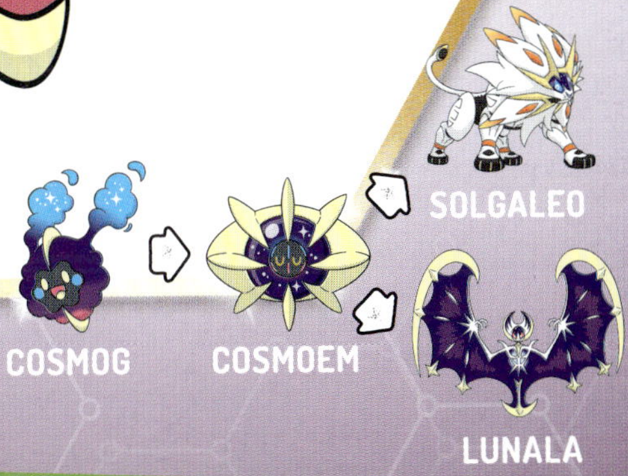

COSMOG

NEBULA POKÉMON
How to Say It: KOZ-mog
Imperial Height: 0'08"
Imperial Weight: 0.2 lbs.
Metric Height: 0.2 m
Metric Weight: 0.1 kg

Type: Psychic
Gender: Unknown
Abilities: Unaware
Weaknesses: Bug, Ghost, Dark

#0488

When it flies, it releases shiny particles from its veil-like wings. It is said to represent the crescent moon.

CRESSELIA

LUNAR POKÉMON
How to Say It: creh-SELL-ee-ah
Imperial Height: 4'11"
Imperial Weight: 188.7 lbs.
Metric Height: 1.5 m
Metric Weight: 85.6 kg

Type: Psychic
Gender: ♀
Abilities: Levitate
Weaknesses: Bug, Ghost, Dark

DOES NOT EVOLVE

#0491

It chases people and Pokémon from its territory by causing them to experience deep, nightmarish slumbers.

It can lull people to sleep and make them dream. It is active during nights of the new moon.

DARKRAI

PITCH-BLACK POKÉMON
How to Say It: DARK-rye
Imperial Height: 4'11"
Imperial Weight: 111.3 lbs.
Metric Height: 1.5 m
Metric Weight: 50.5 kg

Type: Dark
Gender: Unknown
Abilities: Bad Dreams
Weaknesses: Fighting, Bug, Fairy

DOES NOT EVOLVE

#0386

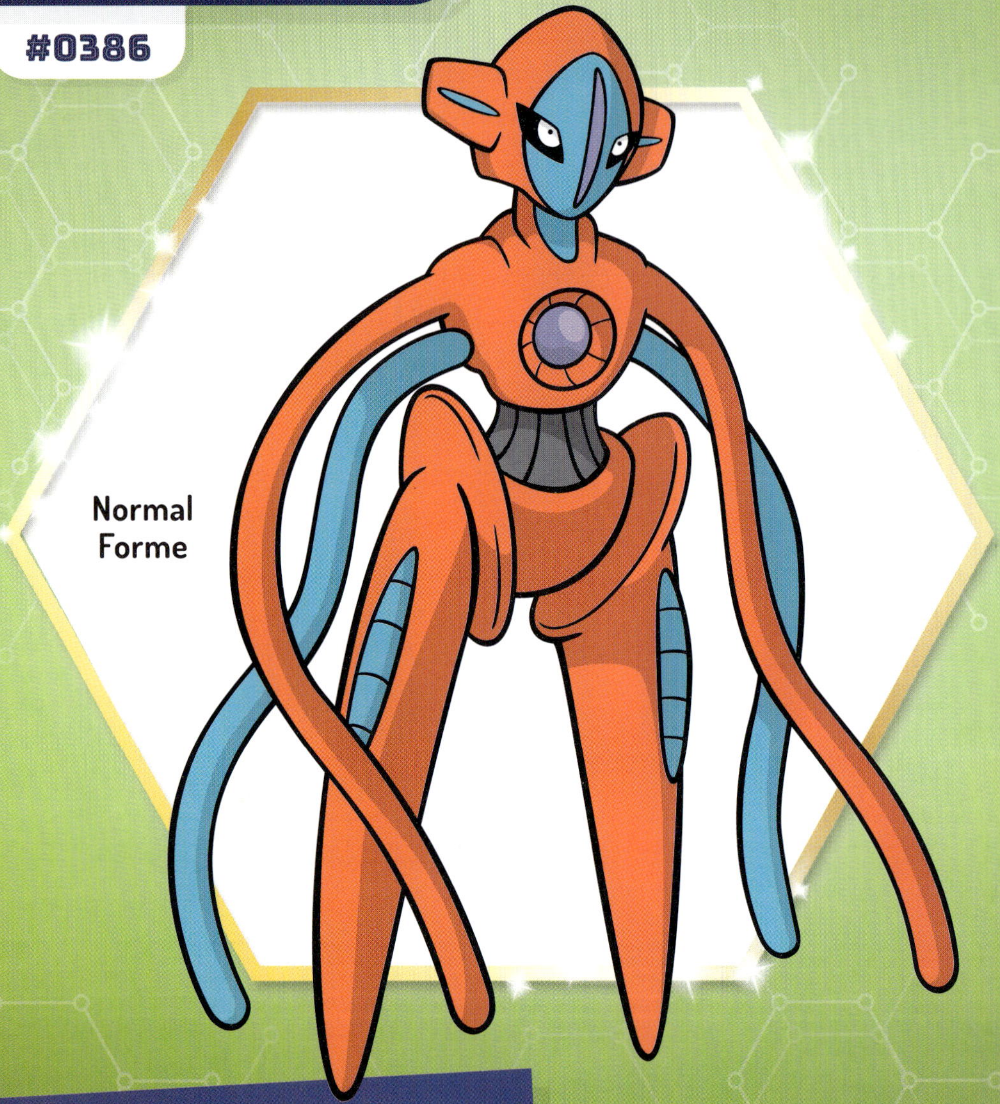

DEOXYS

DNA POKÉMON
How to Say It: dee-OCKS-iss
Imperial Height: 5'07"
Imperial Weight: 134.0 lbs.
Metric Height: 1.7 m
Metric Weight: 60.8 kg

Type: Psychic
Gender: Unknown
Abilities: Pressure
Weaknesses: Bug, Ghost, Dark

DOES NOT EVOLVE

Defense Forme

Attack Forme

Speed Forme

The DNA of a space virus underwent a sudden mutation upon exposure to a laser beam and resulted in Deoxys. The crystalline organ on this Pokémon's chest appears to be its brain.

Deoxys emerged from a virus that came from space. It is highly intelligent and wields psychokinetic powers. This Pokémon shoots lasers from the crystalline organ on its chest.

#0483

It has the power to control time. It appears in Sinnoh-region myths as an ancient deity.

This Pokémon is spoken of in legend. It is said that time began moving when Dialga was born.

DIALGA

TEMPORAL POKÉMON
How to Say It: dee-AWL-gah
Imperial Height: 17'09"
Imperial Weight: 1,505.8 lbs.
Metric Height: 5.4 m
Metric Weight: 683.0 kg

Type: Steel-Dragon
Gender: Unknown
Abilities: Pressure
Weaknesses: Fighting, Ground

DOES NOT EVOLVE

#0483

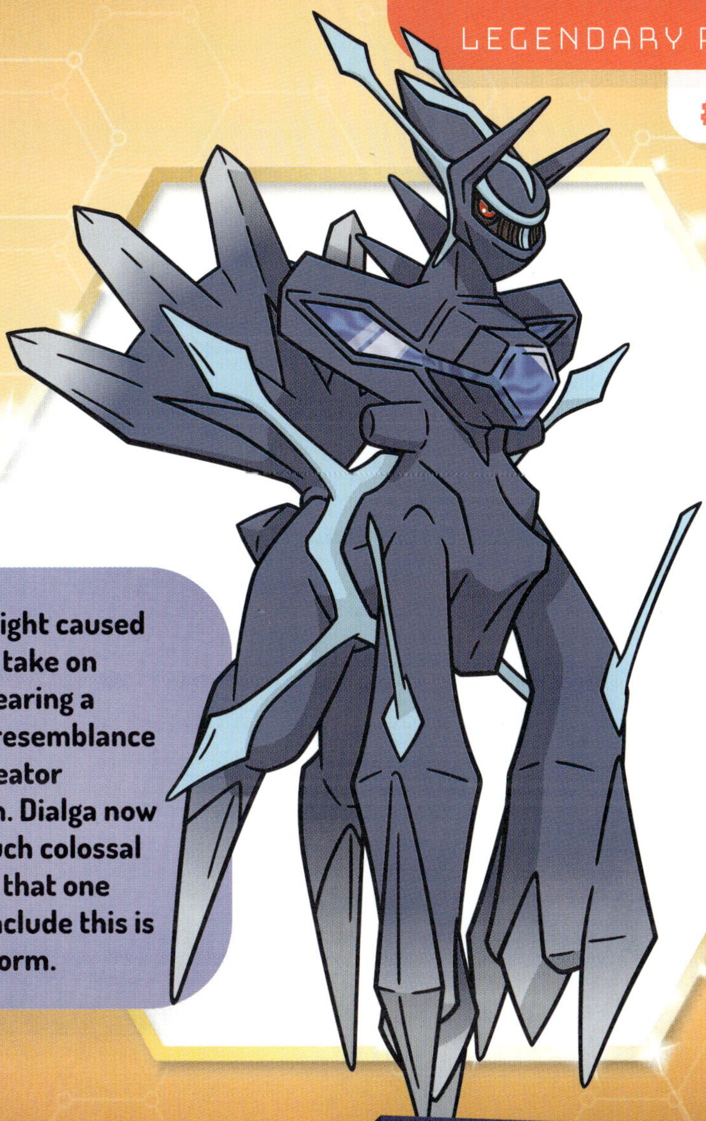

Radiant light caused Dialga to take on a form bearing a striking resemblance to the creator Pokémon. Dialga now wields such colossal strength that one must conclude this is its true form.

ORIGIN FORME
DIALGA

TEMPORAL POKÉMON
How to Say It: dee-AWL-gah
Imperial Height: 23'00"
Imperial Weight: 1,873.9 lbs.
Metric Height: 7.0 m
Metric Weight: 850.0 kg

Type: Steel-Dragon
Gender: Unknown
Abilities: Pressure
Weaknesses: Fighting, Ground

DOES NOT EVOLVE

#0719

A sudden transformation of Carbink, its pink, glimmering body is said to be the loveliest sight in the whole world.

It can instantly create many diamonds by compressing the carbon in the air between its hands.

DIANCIE

JEWEL POKÉMON
How to Say It: die-AHN-see
Imperial Height: 2'04"
Imperial Weight: 19.4 lbs.
Metric Height: 0.7 m
Metric Weight: 8.8 kg

Type: Rock-Fairy
Gender: Unknown
Abilities: Clear Body
Weaknesses: Water, Grass, Ground, Steel

MYTHICAL POKÉMON

#0719

A sudden transformation of Carbink, its pink, glimmering body is said to be the loveliest sight in the whole world.

It can instantly create many diamonds by compressing the carbon in the air between its hands.

DIANCIE MEGA DIANCIE

MEGA DIANCIE

JEWEL POKÉMON
How to Say It: die-AHN-see
Imperial Height: 3'07"
Imperial Weight: 61.3 lbs.
Metric Height: 1.1 m
Metric Weight: 27.8 kg

Type: Rock-Fairy
Gender: Unknown
Abilities: Magic Bounce
Weaknesses: Water, Grass, Ground, Steel

#0905

When it flies to this land from across the sea, the bitter winter comes to an end. According to legend, this Pokémon's love gives rise to the budding of fresh life across Hisui.

INCARNATE FORME

ENAMORUS

LOVE-HATE POKÉMON
How to Say It: eh-NAM-or-us
Imperial Height: 5'03"
Imperial Weight: 105.8 lbs.
Metric Height: 1.6 m
Metric Weight: 48.0 kg

Type: Fairy-Flying
Gender: ♀
Abilities: Cute Charm
Weaknesses: Electric, Ice, Poison, Rock, Steel

DOES NOT EVOLVE

#0905

A different guise from its feminine humanoid form. From the clouds, it descends upon those who treat any form of life with disrespect and metes out wrathful, ruthless punishment.

THERIAN FORME

ENAMORUS

LOVE-HATE POKÉMON
How to Say It: eh-NAM-or-us
Imperial Height: 5'03"
Imperial Weight: 105.8 lbs.
Metric Height: 1.6 m
Metric Weight: 48.0 kg

Type: Fairy-Flying
Gender: ♀
Abilities: Overcoat
Weaknesses: Electric, Ice, Poison, Rock, Steel

DOES NOT EVOLVE

#0244

Entei embodies the passion of magma. This Pokémon is thought to have been born in the eruption of a volcano. It sends up massive bursts of fire that utterly consume all that they touch.

ENTEI

VOLCANO POKÉMON
How to Say It: EN-tay
Imperial Height: 6'11"
Imperial Weight: 436.5 lbs.
Metric Height: 2.1 m
Metric Weight: 198.0 kg

Type: Fire
Gender: Unknown
Abilities: Pressure
Weaknesses: Water, Ground, Rock

DOES NOT EVOLVE

#0890

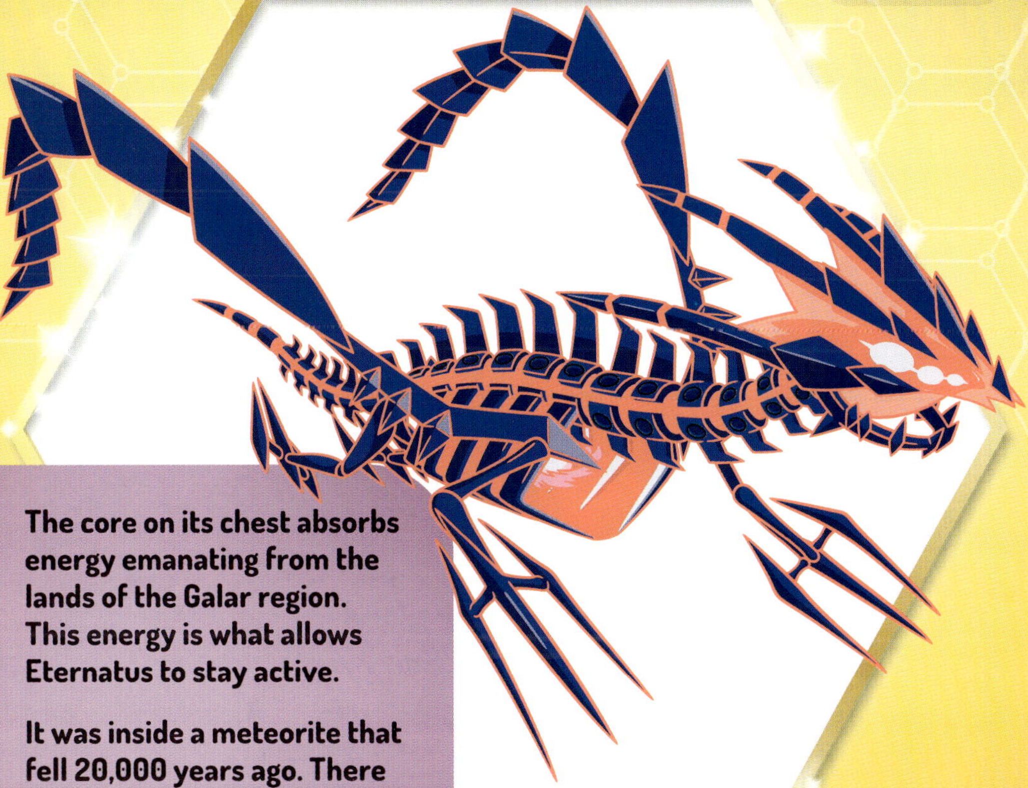

The core on its chest absorbs energy emanating from the lands of the Galar region. This energy is what allows Eternatus to stay active.

It was inside a meteorite that fell 20,000 years ago. There seems to be a connection between this Pokémon and the Dynamax phenomenon.

ETERNATUS

GIGANTIC POKÉMON
How to Say It: ee-TURR-nuh-tuss
Imperial Height: 65'07"
Imperial Weight: 2,094.4 lbs.
Metric Height: 20.0 m
Metric Weight: 950.0 kg

Type: Poison-Dragon
Gender: Unknown
Abilities: Pressure
Weaknesses: Ice, Ground, Psychic, Dragon

DOES NOT EVOLVE

Turn the page to see another form of Eternatus!

#0890

ETERNAMAX

ETERNATUS

GIGANTIC POKÉMON
How to Say It: ee-TURR-nuh-tuss
Imperial Height: 328'01"
Imperial Weight: ?,???.? lbs.
Metric Height: 100.0 m
Metric Weight: ???.? kg

Type: Poison-Dragon
Gender: Unknown
Abilities: Pressure
Weaknesses: Ice, Ground, Psychic, Dragon

DOES NOT EVOLVE

#1016

Fezandipiti owes its beautiful looks and lovely voice to the toxic stimulants emanating from the chain wrapped around its body.

Fezandipiti beats its glossy wings to scatter pheromones that captivate people and Pokémon.

FEZANDIPITI

RETAINER POKÉMON
How to Say It: feh-zun-DIHP-ih-dee
Imperial Height: 4'07"
Imperial Weight: 66.4 lbs.
Metric Height: 1.4 m
Metric Weight: 30.1 kg

Type: Poison-Fairy
Gender: ♂
Abilities: Toxic Chain
Weaknesses: Ground, Psychic, Steel

DOES NOT EVOLVE

#0649

This ancient bug Pokémon was altered by Team Plasma. They upgraded the cannon on its back.

This Pokémon existed 300 million years ago. Team Plasma altered it and attached a cannon to its back.

GENESECT

PALEOZOIC POKÉMON
How to Say It: JEN-uh-sekt
Imperial Height: 4'11"
Imperial Weight: 181.9 lbs.
Metric Height: 1.5 m
Metric Weight: 82.5 kg

Type: Bug-Steel
Gender: Unknown
Abilities: Download
Weaknesses: Fire

DOES NOT EVOLVE

#0487

This Pokémon is said to live in a world on the reverse side of ours, where common knowledge is distorted and strange.

It was banished for its violence. It silently gazed upon the old world from the Distortion World.

ALTERED FORME

GIRATINA

RENEGADE POKÉMON
How to Say It: geer-a-TEE-nuh
Imperial Height: 14'09"
Imperial Weight: 1,653.5 lbs.
Metric Height: 4.5 m
Metric Weight: 750.0 kg

Type: Ghost-Dragon
Gender: Unknown
Abilities: Pressure
Weaknesses: Ice, Ghost, Dragon, Dark, Fairy

DOES NOT EVOLVE

#0487

This Pokémon is said to live in a world on the reverse side of ours, where common knowledge is distorted and strange.

It was banished for its violence. It silently gazed upon the old world from the Distortion World.

ORIGIN FORME

GIRATINA

RENEGADE POKÉMON
How to Say It: geer-a-TEE-nuh
Imperial Height: 22'08"
Imperial Weight: 1,433.0 lbs.
Metric Height: 6.9 m
Metric Weight: 650.0 kg

Type: Ghost-Dragon
Gender: Unknown
Abilities: Levitate
Weaknesses: Ice, Ghost, Dragon, Dark, Fairy

DOES NOT EVOLVE

#0896

Glastrier emits intense cold from its hooves. It's also a belligerent Pokémon—anything it wants, it takes by force.

Glastrier has tremendous physical strength, and the mask of ice covering its face is 100 times harder than diamond.

GLASTRIER

WILD HORSE POKÉMON
How to Say It: GLASS-treer
Imperial Height: 7'03"
Imperial Weight: 1,763.7 lbs.
Metric Height: 2.2 m
Metric Weight: 800.0 kg

Type: Ice
Gender: Unknown
Abilities: Chilling Neigh
Weaknesses: Fire, Fighting, Rock, Steel

DOES NOT EVOLVE

#0383

Groudon is said to be the personification of the land itself. Legends tell of its many clashes against Kyogre, as each sought to gain the power of nature.

Through Primal Reversion and with nature's full power, it will take back its true form. It can cause magma to erupt and expand the landmass of the world.

GROUDON

CONTINENT POKÉMON
How to Say It: GRAU-DON
Imperial Height: 11'06"
Imperial Weight: 2,094.4 lbs.
Metric Height: 3.5 m
Metric Weight: 950.0 kg

Type: Ground
Gender: Unknown
Abilities: Drought
Weaknesses: Water, Grass, Ice

DOES NOT EVOLVE

Turn the page to see another form of Groudon!

#0383

Groudon is said to be the personification of the land itself. Legends tell of its many clashes against Kyogre, as each sought to gain the power of nature.

Through Primal Reversion and with nature's full power, it will take back its true form. It can cause magma to erupt and expand the landmass of the world.

PRIMAL GROUDON

CONTINENT POKÉMON
How to Say It: GRAU-DON
Imperial Height: 16'05"
Imperial Weight: 2,204.0 lbs.
Metric Height: 5.0 m
Metric Weight: 999.7 kg

Type: Ground-Fire
Gender: Unknown
Abilities: Desolate Land
Weaknesses: Water, Ground

DOES NOT EVOLVE

#0485

It dwells in volcanic caves. It digs in with its cross-shaped feet to crawl on ceilings and walls.

Boiling blood, like magma, circulates through its body. It makes its dwelling place in volcanic caves.

HEATRAN

LAVA DOME POKÉMON
How to Say It: HEET-tran
Imperial Height: 5'07"
Imperial Weight: 948.0 lbs.
Metric Height: 1.7 m
Metric Weight: 430.0 kg

Type: Fire-Steel
Gender: ♂ ♀
Abilities: Flash Fire
Weaknesses: Water, Fighting, Ground

DOES NOT EVOLVE

#0250

Ho-Oh's feathers glow in seven colors depending on the angle at which they are struck by light. These feathers are said to bring happiness to the bearers. This Pokémon is said to live at the foot of a rainbow.

HO-OH

RAINBOW POKÉMON
How to Say It: HOE-OH
Imperial Height: 12'06"
Imperial Weight: 438.7 lbs.
Metric Height: 3.8 m
Metric Weight: 199.0 kg

Type: Fire-Flying
Gender: Unknown
Abilities: Pressure
Weaknesses: Water, Electric, Rock

DOES NOT EVOLVE

#0720

In its true form, it possesses a huge amount of power. Legends of its avarice tell how it once carried off an entire castle to gain the treasure hidden within.

It is said to be able to seize anything it desires with its six rings and six huge arms. With its power sealed, it is transformed into a much smaller form.

HOOPA

CONFINED

MISCHIEF POKÉMON
How to Say It: HOO-pah
Imperial Height: 1'08"
Imperial Weight: 19.8 lbs.
Metric Height: 0.5 m
Metric Weight: 9.0 kg

Type: Psychic-Ghost
Gender: Unknown
Abilities: Magician
Weaknesses: Ghost, Dark

DOES NOT EVOLVE

Turn the page to see another form of Hoopa!

#0720

In its true form, it possesses a huge amount of power. Legends of its avarice tell how it once carried off an entire castle to gain the treasure hidden within.

It is said to be able to seize anything it desires with its six rings and six huge arms. With its power sealed, it is transformed into a much smaller form.

HOOPA

UNBOUND

DJINN POKÉMON
How to Say It: HOO-pah
Imperial Height: 21'04"
Imperial Weight: 1,080.3 lbs.
Metric Height: 6.5 m
Metric Weight: 490.0 kg

Type: Psychic-Dark
Gender: Unknown
Abilities: Magician
Weaknesses: Bug, Fairy

DOES NOT EVOLVE

#0385

A legend states that Jirachi will make true any wish that is written on notes attached to its head when it awakens. If this Pokémon senses danger, it will fight without awakening.

Jirachi will awaken from its sleep of a thousand years if you sing to it in a voice of purity. It is said to make true any wish that people desire.

JIRACHI

WISH POKÉMON
How to Say It: jir-AH-chi
Imperial Height: 1'00"
Imperial Weight: 2.4 lbs.
Metric Height: 0.3 m
Metric Weight: 1.1 kg

Type: Steel-Psychic
Gender: Unknown
Abilities: Serene Grace
Weaknesses: Fire, Ground, Ghost, Dark

DOES NOT EVOLVE

#0647

It crosses the world, running over the surfaces of oceans and rivers. It appears at scenic waterfronts.

When it is resolute, its body fills with power and it becomes swifter. Its jumps are then too fast to follow.

ORDINARY FORM

KELDEO

COLT POKÉMON
How to Say It: KELL-dee-oh
Imperial Height: 4'07"
Imperial Weight: 160.9 lbs.
Metric Height: 1.4 m
Metric Weight: 48.5 kg

Type: Water-Fighting
Gender: Unknown
Abilities: Justified
Weaknesses: Grass, Electric, Flying, Psychic, Fairy

DOES NOT EVOLVE

#0647

It crosses the world, running over the surfaces of oceans and rivers. It appears at scenic waterfronts.

When it is resolute, its body fills with power and it becomes swifter. Its jumps are then too fast to follow.

RESOLUTE FORM

KELDEO

COLT POKÉMON
How to Say It: KELL-dee-oh
Imperial Height: 4'07"
Imperial Weight: 160.9 lbs.
Metric Height: 1.4 m
Metric Weight: 48.5 kg

Type: Water-Fighting
Gender: Unknown
Abilities: Justified
Weaknesses: Grass, Electric, Flying, Psychic, Fairy

DOES NOT EVOLVE

#1007

This seems to be the Winged King mentioned in an old expedition journal. It was said to have split the land with its bare fists.

This Pokémon resembles Cyclizar, but it is far burlier and more ferocious. Nothing is known about its ecology or other features.

KORAIDON

PARADOX POKÉMON
How to Say It: koh-RAI-dahn
Imperial Height: 8'02"
Imperial Weight: 668.0 lbs.
Metric Height: 2.5 m
Metric Weight: 303.0 kg

Type: Fighting-Dragon
Gender: Unknown
Abilities: Orichalcum Pulse
Weaknesses: Psychic, Flying, Fairy, Ice, Dragon

DOES NOT EVOLVE

#0891

Kubfu trains hard to perfect its moves. The moves it masters will determine which form it takes when it evolves.

If Kubfu pulls the long white hair on its head, its fighting spirit heightens and power wells up from the depths of its belly.

KUBFU

WUSHU POKÉMON
How to Say It: kub-foo
Imperial Height: 2'00"
Imperial Weight: 26.5 lbs.
Metric Height: 0.6 m
Metric Weight: 12.0 kg

Type: Fighting
Gender: ♂ ♀
Abilities: Inner Focus
Weaknesses: Flying, Psychic, Fairy

#0382

Through Primal Reversion and with nature's full power, it will take back its true form. It can summon storms that cause the sea levels to rise.

Kyogre is said to be the personification of the sea itself. Legends tell of its many clashes against Groudon, as each sought to gain the power of nature.

KYOGRE

SEA BASIN POKÉMON
How to Say It: kai-OH-gurr
Imperial Height: 14'09"
Imperial Weight: 776.0 lbs.
Metric Height: 4.5 m
Metric Weight: 352.0 kg

Type: Water
Gender: Unknown
Abilities: Drizzle
Weaknesses: Grass, Electric

DOES NOT EVOLVE

#0382

Through Primal Reversion and with nature's full power, it will take back its true form. It can summon storms that cause the sea levels to rise.

Kyogre is said to be the personification of the sea itself. Legends tell of its many clashes against Groudon, as each sought to gain the power of nature.

PRIMAL KYOGRE

SEA BASIN POKÉMON
How to Say It: kai-OH-gurr
Imperial Height: 32'02"
Imperial Weight: 948.0 lbs.
Metric Height: 9.8 m
Metric Weight: 430.0 kg

Type: Water
Gender: Unknown
Abilities: Primordial Sea
Weaknesses: Grass, Electric

DOES NOT EVOLVE

#0646

This legendary ice Pokémon waits for a hero to fill in the missing parts of its body with truth or ideals.

It generates a powerful, freezing energy inside itself, but its body became frozen when the energy leaked out.

KYUREM

BOUNDARY POKÉMON
How to Say It: KYOO-rem
Imperial Height: 9'10"
Imperial Weight: 716.5 lbs.
Metric Height: 3.0 m
Metric Weight: 325.0 kg

Type: Dragon-Ice
Gender: Unknown
Abilities: Pressure
Weaknesses: Fighting, Rock, Dragon, Steel, Fairy

DOES NOT EVOLVE

#0646

This legendary ice Pokémon waits for a hero to fill in the missing parts of its body with truth or ideals.

It generates a powerful, freezing energy inside itself, but its body became frozen when the energy leaked out.

BLACK KYUREM

BOUNDARY POKÉMON
How to Say It: KYOO-rem
Imperial Height: 10'10"
Imperial Weight: 716.5 lbs.
Metric Height: 3.3 m
Metric Weight: 325.0 kg

Type: Dragon-Ice
Gender: Unknown
Abilities: Teravolt
Weaknesses: Fighting, Rock, Dragon, Steel, Fairy

DOES NOT EVOLVE

Turn the page to see another form of Kyurem!

#0646

This legendary ice Pokémon waits for a hero to fill in the missing parts of its body with truth or ideals.

It generates a powerful, freezing energy inside itself, but its body became frozen when the energy leaked out.

WHITE KYUREM

BOUNDARY POKÉMON
How to Say It: KYOO-rem
Imperial Height: 11'10"
Imperial Weight: 716.5 lbs.
Metric Height: 3.6 m
Metric Weight: 325.0 kg

Type: Dragon-Ice
Gender: Unknown
Abilities: Turboblaze
Weaknesses: Fighting, Rock, Dragon, Steel, Fairy

DOES NOT EVOLVE

#0645

Lands visited by Landorus grant such bountiful crops that it has been hailed as "The Guardian of the Fields."

From the forces of lightning and wind, it creates energy to give nutrients to the soil and make the land abundant.

INCARNATE FORME

LANDORUS

ABUNDANCE POKÉMON
How to Say It: LAN-duh-rus
Imperial Height: 4'11"
Imperial Weight: 149.9 lbs.
Metric Height: 1.5 m
Metric Weight: 68.0 kg

Type: Ground-Flying
Gender: ♂
Abilities: Sand Force
Weaknesses: Water, Ice

DOES NOT EVOLVE

Turn the page to see another form of Landorus!

#0645

Lands visited by Landorus grant such bountiful crops that it has been hailed as "The Guardian of the Fields."

From the forces of lightning and wind, it creates energy to give nutrients to the soil and make the land abundant.

THERIAN FORME

LANDORUS

ABUNDANCE POKÉMON
How to Say It: LAN-duh-rus
Imperial Height: 4'03"
Imperial Weight: 149.9 lbs.
Metric Height: 1.3 m
Metric Weight: 68.0 kg

Type: Ground-Flying
Gender: ♂
Abilities: Intimidate
Weaknesses: Water, Ice

DOES NOT EVOLVE

#0380

Latias is highly sensitive to the emotions of people. If it senses any hostility, this Pokémon ruffles the feathers all over its body and cries shrilly to intimidate the foe.

Latias is highly intelligent and capable of understanding human speech. It is covered with a glass-like down. The Pokémon enfolds its body with its down and refracts light to alter its appearance.

LATIAS MEGA LATIAS

LATIAS

EON POKÉMON
How to Say It: LAT-ee-ahs
Imperial Height: 4'07"
Imperial Weight: 88.2 lbs.
Metric Height: 1.4 m
Metric Weight: 40.0 kg

Type: Dragon-Psychic
Gender: ♀
Abilities: Levitate
Weaknesses: Ice, Bug, Ghost, Dragon, Dark, Fairy

Turn the page to see the Mega Evolution of Latias!

#0380

Latias is highly sensitive to the emotions of people. If it senses any hostility, this Pokémon ruffles the feathers all over its body and cries shrilly to intimidate the foe.

Latias is highly intelligent and capable of understanding human speech. It is covered with a glass-like down. The Pokémon enfolds its body with its down and refracts light to alter its appearance.

LATIAS MEGA LATIAS

MEGA LATIAS

EON POKÉMON
How to Say It: LAT-ee-ahs
Imperial Height: 5'11"
Imperial Weight: 114.6 lbs.
Metric Height: 1.8 m
Metric Weight: 52.0 kg

Type: Dragon-Psychic
Gender: ♀
Abilities: Levitate
Weaknesses: Ice, Bug, Ghost, Dragon, Dark, Fairy

#0381

Latios has the ability to make others see an image of what it has seen or imagines in its head. This Pokémon is intelligent and understands human speech.

Latios will only open its heart to a Trainer with a compassionate spirit. This Pokémon can fly faster than a jet plane by folding its forelegs to minimize air resistance.

LATIOS MEGA LATIOS

LATIOS

EON POKÉMON
How to Say It: LAT-ee-ose
Imperial Height: 6'07"
Imperial Weight: 132.3 lbs.
Metric Height: 2.0 m
Metric Weight: 60.0 kg

Type: Dragon-Psychic
Gender: ♂
Abilities: Levitate
Weaknesses: Ice, Bug, Ghost, Dragon, Dark, Fairy

Turn the page to see the Mega Evolution of Latios!

#0381

LATIOS MEGA LATIOS

Latios has the ability to make others see an image of what it has seen or imagines in its head. This Pokémon is intelligent and understands human speech.

Latios will only open its heart to a Trainer with a compassionate spirit. This Pokémon can fly faster than a jet plane by folding its forelegs to minimize air resistance.

MEGA LATIOS

EON POKÉMON

How to Say It: LAT-ee-ose

Imperial Height: 7'07"

Imperial Weight: 154.3 lbs.

Metric Height: 2.3 m

Metric Weight: 70.0 kg

Type: Dragon-Psychic

Gender: ♂

Abilities: Levitate

Weaknesses: Ice, Bug, Ghost, Dragon, Dark, Fairy

#0249

Lugia's wings pack devastating power—a light fluttering of its wings can blow apart regular houses. As a result, this Pokémon chooses to live out of sight deep under the sea.

LUGIA

DIVING POKÉMON
How to Say It: LOO-gee-uh
Imperial Height: 17'01"
Imperial Weight: 476.2 lbs.
Metric Height: 5.2 m
Metric Weight: 216.0 kg

Type: Psychic-Flying
Gender: Unknown
Abilities: Pressure
Weaknesses: Electric, Ice, Rock, Ghost, Dark

DOES NOT EVOLVE

#0792

Records of it exist in writings from long, long ago, where it was known by the name "the beast that calls the moon."

It sometimes summons unknown powers and life-forms here to this world from holes that lead to other worlds.

LUNALA

MOONE POKÉMON
How to Say It: loo-NAH-luh
Imperial Height: 13'01"
Imperial Weight: 264.6 lbs.
Metric Height: 4.0 m
Metric Weight: 120.0 kg

Type: Psychic-Ghost
Gender: Unknown
Abilities: Shadow Shield
Weaknesses: Ghost, Dark

#0801

It synchronizes its consciousness with others to understand their feelings. This faculty makes it useful for taking care of people.

Built roughly 500 years ago by a scientist, the part called the Soul-Heart is the actual life-form.

MAGEARNA

ARTIFICIAL POKÉMON
How to Say It: muh-GEER-buh
Imperial Height: 3'03"
Imperial Weight: 177.5 lbs.
Metric Height: 1.0 m
Metric Weight: 80.5 kg

Type: Steel-Fairy
Gender: Unknown
Abilities: Soul-Heart
Weaknesses: Fire, Ground

DOES NOT EVOLVE

#0490

It is born with a wondrous power that lets it bond with any kind of Pokémon.

It starts its life with a wondrous power that permits it to bond with any kind of Pokémon.

MANAPHY

SEAFARING POKÉMON
How to Say It: MAN-ah-fee
Imperial Height: 1'00"
Imperial Weight: 3.1 lbs.
Metric Height: 0.3 m
Metric Weight: 1.4 kg

Type: Water
Gender: Unknown
Abilities: Hydration
Weaknesses: Grass, Electric

DOES NOT EVOLVE

#0802

It slips into the shadows of others and mimics their powers and movements. As it improves, it becomes stronger than those it's imitating.

It sinks into the shadows of people and Pokémon, where it can understand their feelings and copy their capabilities.

MARSHADOW

GLOOMDWELLER POKÉMON
How to Say It: mar-SHAD-oh
Imperial Height: 2'04"
Imperial Weight: 48.9 lbs.
Metric Height: 0.7 m
Metric Weight: 22.2 kg

Type: Fighting-Ghost
Gender: Unknown
Abilities: Technician
Weaknesses: Flying, Psychic, Ghost, Fairy

DOES NOT EVOLVE

#0809

At the end of its lifespan, Melmetal will rust and fall apart. The small shards left behind will eventually be reborn as Meltan.

Centrifugal force is behind the punches of Melmetal's heavy hex-nut arms. Melmetal is said to deliver the strongest punches of all Pokémon.

MELTAN MELMETAL

MELMETAL

HEX NUT POKÉMON
How to Say It: MEL-metal
Imperial Height: 8'02"
Imperial Weight: 1,763.7 lbs.
Metric Height: 2.5 m
Metric Weight: 800.0 kg

Type: Steel
Gender: Unknown
Abilities: Iron Fist
Weaknesses: Fire, Fighting, Ground

#0809

In a distant land, there are legends about a cyclopean giant. In fact, the giant was a Melmetal that was flooded with Gigantamax energy.

It can send electric beams streaking out from the hole in its belly. The beams' tremendous energy can vaporize an opponent in one shot.

MELTAN MELMETAL

GIGANTAMAX MELMETAL

HEX NUT POKÉMON
How to Say It: MEL-metal
Imperial Height: 82'00"+
Imperial Weight: ?,???.? lbs.
Metric Height: 25.0+ m
Metric Weight: ???.? kg

Type: Steel
Gender: Unknown
Abilities: Iron Fist
Weaknesses: Fire, Fighting, Ground

#0648

The melodies sung by Meloetta have the power to make Pokémon that hear them happy or sad.

Its melodies are sung with a special vocalization method that can control the feelings of those who hear it.

ARIA FORME

MELOETTA

MELODY POKÉMON
How to Say It: mell-oh-ET-tuh
Imperial Height: 2'00"
Imperial Weight: 14.3 lbs.
Metric Height: 0.6 m
Metric Weight: 6.5 kg

Type: Normal-Psychic
Gender: Unknown
Abilities: Serene Grace
Weaknesses: Bug, Dark

DOES NOT EVOLVE

MYTHICAL POKÉMON

#0648

The melodies sung by Meloetta have the power to make Pokémon that hear them happy or sad.

Its melodies are sung with a special vocalization method that can control the feelings of those who hear it.

PIROUETTE FORME

MELOETTA

MELODY POKÉMON
How to Say It: mell-oh-ET-tuh
Imperial Height: 2'00"
Imperial Weight: 14.3 lbs.
Metric Height: 0.6 m
Metric Weight: 6.5 kg

Type: Normal-Fighting
Gender: Unknown
Abilities: Serene Grace
Weaknesses: Fighting, Flying, Psychic, Fairy

DOES NOT EVOLVE

#0808

It melts particles of iron and other metals found in the subsoil, so it can absorb them into its body of molten steel.

MELTAN

HEX NUT POKÉMON
How to Say It: MEL-tan
Imperial Height: 0'08"
Imperial Weight: 17.6 lbs.
Metric Height: 0.2 m
Metric Weight: 8.0 kg

Type: Steel
Gender: Unknown
Abilities: Magnet Pull
Weaknesses: Fire, Fighting, Ground

#0481

Known as "The Being of Emotion." It taught humans the nobility of sorrow, pain, and joy.

It sleeps at the bottom of a lake. Its spirit is said to leave its body to fly on the lake's surface.

MESPRIT

EMOTION POKÉMON
How to Say It: MESS-sprit
Imperial Height: 1'00"
Imperial Weight: 0.7 lbs.
Metric Height: 0.3 m
Metric Weight: 0.3 kg

Type: Psychic
Gender: Unknown
Abilities: Levitate
Weaknesses: Bug, Ghost, Dark

DOES NOT EVOLVE

#0151

When viewed through a microscope, this Pokémon's short, fine, delicate hair can be seen.

MEW

NEW SPECIES POKÉMON
How to Say It: MUE
Imperial Height: 1'04"
Imperial Weight: 8.8 lbs.
Metric Height: 0.4 m
Metric Weight: 4.0 kg

Type: Psychic
Gender: Unknown
Abilities: Synchronize
Weaknesses: Bug, Ghost, Dark

DOES NOT EVOLVE

#0150

Its DNA is almost the same as Mew's. However, its size and disposition are vastly different.

MEWTWO

GENETIC POKÉMON
How to Say It: MUE-TOO
Imperial Height: 6'07"
Imperial Weight: 269.0 lbs.
Metric Height: 2.0 m
Metric Weight: 122.0 kg

Type: Psychic
Gender: Unknown
Abilities: Pressure
Weaknesses: Bug, Ghost, Dark

Turn the page to see the Mega Evolutions of Mewtwo!

#0150

Psychic power has augmented its muscles. It has a grip strength of one ton and can sprint a hundred meters in two seconds flat!

MEGA MEWTWO X

GENETIC POKÉMON
How to Say It: MUE-TOO
Imperial Height: 7'07"
Imperial Weight: 280.0 lbs.
Metric Height: 2.3 m
Metric Weight: 127.0 kg

Type: Psychic-Fighting
Gender: Unknown
Abilities: Steadfast
Weaknesses: Flying, Ghost, Fairy

LEGENDARY POKÉMON

#0150

Despite its diminished size, its mental power has grown phenomenally. With a mere thought, it can smash a skyscraper to smithereens.

MEGA MEWTWO Y

GENETIC POKÉMON
How to Say It: MUE-TOO
Imperial Height: 4'11"
Imperial Weight: 72.8 lbs.
Metric Height: 1.5 m
Metric Weight: 33.0 kg

Type: Psychic
Gender: Unknown
Abilities: Insomnia
Weaknesses: Bug, Ghost, Dark

#1008

Much remains unknown about this creature. It resembles Cyclizar, but it is far more ruthless and powerful.

This seems to be the Iron Serpent mentioned in an old book. The Iron Serpent is said to have turned the land to ash with its lightning.

MIRAIDON

PARADOX POKÉMON
How to Say It: meer-RAI-dahn
Imperial Height: 11'06"
Imperial Weight: 529.1 lbs.
Metric Height: 3.5 m
Metric Weight: 240.0 kg

Type: Electric-Dragon
Gender: Unknown
Abilities: Hadron Engine
Weaknesses: Fairy, Ground, Ice, Dragon

DOES NOT EVOLVE

#0146

It is one of the legendary bird Pokémon. Its appearance is said to indicate the coming of spring.

MOLTRES

FLAME POKÉMON
How to Say It: MOHL-trace
Imperial Height: 6'07"
Imperial Weight: 132.3 lbs.
Metric Height: 2.0 m
Metric Weight: 60.0 kg

Type: Fire-Flying
Gender: Unknown
Abilities: Pressure
Weaknesses: Water, Electric, Rock

DOES NOT EVOLVE

Turn the page to see a regional form of Moltres!

#0146

This Pokémon's sinister, flame-like aura will consume the spirit of any creature it hits. Victims become burned-out shadows of themselves.

The sinister aura that blazes like molten fire around this Pokémon is what inspired the name Moltres.

GALARIAN MOLTRES

MALEVOLENT POKÉMON
How to Say It: MOHL-trace
Imperial Height: 6'07"
Imperial Weight: 145.5 lbs.
Metric Height: 2.0 m
Metric Weight: 66.0 kg

Type: Dark-Flying
Gender: Unknown
Abilities: Berserk
Weaknesses: Fairy, Electric, Ice, Rock

DOES NOT EVOLVE

#1015

The chain is made from toxins that enhance capabilities. It stimulated Munkidori's brain and caused the Pokémon's psychic powers to bloom.

Munkidori keeps itself somewhere safe while it toys with its foes, using psychokinesis to induce intense dizziness.

MUNKIDORI

RETAINER POKÉMON
How to Say It: MUHN-kee-DOR-ee
Imperial Height: 3'03"
Imperial Weight: 26.9 lbs.
Metric Height: 1.0 m
Metric Weight: 12.2 kg

Type: Poison-Psychic
Gender: ♂
Abilities: Toxic Chain
Weaknesses: Ground, Ghost, Dark

DOES NOT EVOLVE

#0800

It looks somehow pained as it rages around in search of light, which serves as its energy. It's apparently from another world.

Light is the source of its energy. If it isn't devouring light, impurities build up in it and on it, and Necrozma darkens and stops moving.

NECROZMA

PRISM POKÉMON
How to Say It: neh-KROHZ-muh
Imperial Height: 7'10"
Imperial Weight: 507.1 lbs.
Metric Height: 2.4 m
Metric Weight: 230.0 kg

Type: Psychic
Gender: Unknown
Abilities: Prism Armor
Weaknesses: Bug, Ghost, Dark

DOES NOT EVOLVE

#0800

Lunala no longer has a will of its own. Now under the control of Necrozma, it continuously expels all its energy.

This is its form while it's devouring the light of Lunala. It grasps foes in its giant claws and rips them apart with brute force.

DAWN WINGS

NECROZMA

PRISM POKÉMON
How to Say It: neh-KROHZ-muh
Imperial Height: 13'09"
Imperial Weight: 771.6 lbs.
Metric Height: 4.2 m
Metric Weight: 350.0 kg

Type: Psychic-Ghost
Gender: Unknown
Abilities: Prism Armor
Weaknesses: Ghost, Dark

DOES NOT EVOLVE

Turn the page to see more forms of Necrozma!

#0800

This is its form while it is devouring the light of Solgaleo. It pounces on foes and then slashes them with the claws on its four limbs and back.

This is Necrozma's form while it's absorbing the power of Solgaleo, making it extremely ferocious and impossible to control.

DUSK MANE

NECROZMA

PRISM POKÉMON
How to Say It: neh-KROHZ-muh
Imperial Height: 12'06"
Imperial Weight: 1,014.1 lbs.
Metric Height: 3.8 m
Metric Weight: 460.0 kg

Type: Psychic-Steel
Gender: Unknown
Abilities: Prism Armor
Weaknesses: Fire, Ground, Ghost, Dark

DOES NOT EVOLVE

#0800

This is its form when it has absorbed overwhelming light energy. It fires laser beams from all over its body.

The light pouring out from all over its body affects living things and nature, impacting them in various ways.

ULTRA NECROZMA

PRISM POKÉMON
How to Say It: neh-KROHZ-muh
Imperial Height: 24'07"
Imperial Weight: 507.1 lbs.
Metric Height: 7.5 m
Metric Weight: 230.0 kg

Type: Psychic-Dragon
Gender: Unknown
Abilities: Neuroforce
Weaknesses: Ice, Bug, Ghost, Dragon, Dark, Fairy

DOES NOT EVOLVE

#1017

This Pokémon's type changes based on which mask it's wearing. It confounds its enemies with nimble movements and kicks.

This mischief-loving Pokémon is full of curiosity. It battles by drawing out the type-based energy contained within its masks.

TEAL MASK

OGERPON

MASK POKÉMON
How to Say It: OH-gur-pahn
Imperial Height: 3'11"
Imperial Weight: 87.7 lbs.
Metric Height: 1.2 m
Metric Weight: 39.8 kg

Type: Grass
Gender: ♀
Abilities: Defiant
Weaknesses: Fire, Ice, Poison, Flying, Bug

DOES NOT EVOLVE

TEAL MASK OGERPON TERASTALLIZED

Turn the page to see more forms of Ogerpon!

#1017

This form has excellent defenses, absorbing impacts solidly like the cornerstones that support houses.

In this form, it draws on the power of stone. Its body is rock-solid, protecting it from all manner of attacks.

CORNERSTONE MASK

OGERPON

MASK POKÉMON
How to Say It: OH-gur-pahn
Imperial Height: 3'11"
Imperial Weight: 87.7 lbs.
Metric Height: 1.2 m
Metric Weight: 39.8 kg

Type: Grass-Rock
Gender: ♀
Abilities: Sturdy
Weaknesses: Ice, Fighting, Bug, Steel

DOES NOT EVOLVE

CORNERSTONE MASK OGERPON TERASTALLIZED

Turn the page to see more forms of Ogerpon!

#1017

This form is the most aggressive, bombarding enemies with the intensity of flames blazing within a hearth.

In this form, it draws on the power of fire. It spears its enemies with thorn-covered ivy.

HEARTHFLAME MASK OGERPON

MASK POKÉMON
How to Say It: OH-gur-pahn
Imperial Height: 3'11"
Imperial Weight: 87.7 lbs.
Metric Height: 1.2 m
Metric Weight: 39.8 kg

Type: Grass-Fire
Gender: ♀
Abilities: Mold Breaker
Weaknesses: Poison, Flying, Rock

DOES NOT EVOLVE

HEARTHFLAME MASK OGERPON TERASTALLIZED

Turn the page to see more forms of Ogerpon!

#1017

This form excels in both attack and defense. It ceaselessly unleashes moves like a spring gushes water.

In this form, it draws on the power of water. It attacks unrelentingly with kicks and ivy strikes.

WELLSPRING MASK

OGERPON

MASK POKÉMON
How to Say It: OH-gur-pahn
Imperial Height: 3'11"
Imperial Weight: 87.7 lbs.
Metric Height: 1.2 m
Metric Weight: 39.8 kg

Type: Grass-Water
Gender: ♀
Abilities: Water Absorb
Weaknesses: Poison, Flying, Bug

DOES NOT EVOLVE

WELLSPRING MASK
OGERPON TERASTALLIZED

#1014

After all its muscles were stimulated by the toxic chain around its neck, Okidogi transformed and gained a powerful physique.

Okidogi is a ruffian with a short temper. It can pulverize anything by swinging around the chain on its neck.

OKIDOGI

RETAINER POKÉMON
How to Say It: OH-kee-DOH-gee
Imperial Height: 5'11"
Imperial Weight: 203.3 lbs.
Metric Height: 1.8 m
Metric Weight: 92.2 kg

Type: Poison-Fighting
Gender: ♂
Abilities: Toxic Chain
Weaknesses: Ground, Flying, Psychic

DOES NOT EVOLVE

#0484

It has the ability to distort space. It is described as a deity in Sinnoh-region mythology.

It is said to live in a gap in the spatial dimension parallel to ours. Palkia appears in mythology.

PALKIA

SPATIAL POKÉMON
How to Say It: PALL-kee-ah
Imperial Height: 13'09"
Imperial Weight: 740.8 lbs.
Metric Height: 4.2 m
Metric Weight: 336.0 kg

Type: Water-Dragon
Gender: Unknown
Abilities: Pressure
Weaknesses: Dragon, Fairy

DOES NOT EVOLVE

Turn the page to see another form of Palkia!

LEGENDARY POKÉMON

#0484

It soars across the sky in a form that greatly resembles the creator of all things. Perhaps this imitation of appearance is Palkia's strategy for gaining Arceus's powers.

ORIGIN FORME

PALKIA

SPATIAL POKÉMON
How to Say It: PALL-kee-ah
Imperial Height: 20'08"
Imperial Weight: 1,455.1 lbs.
Metric Height: 6.3 m
Metric Weight: 660.0 kg

Type: Water-Dragon
Gender: Unknown
Abilities: Pressure
Weaknesses: Dragon, Fairy

DOES NOT EVOLVE

#1025

It feeds others toxic mochi that draw out desires and capabilities. Those who eat the mochi fall under Pecharunt's control, chained to its will.

Its peach-shaped shell serves as storage for a potent poison. It makes poisonous mochi and serves them to people and Pokémon.

PECHARUNT

SUBJUGATION POKÉMON
How to Say It: PEH-chuh-ruhnt
Imperial Height: 1'00"
Imperial Weight: 0.7 lbs.
Metric Height: 0.3 m
Metric Weight: 0.3 kg

Type: Poison-Ghost
Gender: Unknown
Abilities: Poison Puppeteer
Weaknesses: Ground, Psychic, Ghost, Dark

DOES NOT EVOLVE

#0489

When the water warms, they inflate the flotation sac on their heads and drift languidly on the sea in packs.

It drifts in warm seas. It always returns to where it was born, no matter how far it may have drifted.

PHIONE

SEA DRIFTER POKÉMON
How to Say It: fee-OH-nay
Imperial Height: 1'04"
Imperial Weight: 6.8 lbs.
Metric Height: 0.4 m
Metric Weight: 3.1 kg

Type: Water
Gender: Unknown
Abilities: Hydration
Weaknesses: Grass, Electric

DOES NOT EVOLVE

#0243

Raikou embodies the speed of lightning. The roars of this Pokémon send shock waves shuddering through the air and shake the ground as if lightning bolts had come crashing down.

RAIKOU

THUNDER POKÉMON
How to Say It: RYE-koh
Imperial Height: 6'03"
Imperial Weight: 392.4 lbs.
Metric Height: 1.9 m
Metric Weight: 178.0 kg

Type: Electric
Gender: Unknown
Abilities: Pressure
Weaknesses: Ground

DOES NOT EVOLVE

#0384

Rayquaza is said to have lived for hundreds of millions of years. Legends remain of how it put to rest the clash between Kyogre and Groudon.

It flies forever through the ozone layer, consuming meteoroids for sustenance. The many meteoroids in its body provide the energy it needs to Mega Evolve.

RAYQUAZA MEGA RAYQUAZA

RAYQUAZA

SKY HIGH POKÉMON
How to Say It: ray-KWAY-zuh
Imperial Height: 23'00"
Imperial Weight: 455.3 lbs.
Metric Height: 7.0 m
Metric Weight: 206.5 kg

Type: Dragon-Flying
Gender: Unknown
Abilities: Air Lock
Weaknesses: Ice, Rock, Dragon, Fairy

#0384

Rayquaza is said to have lived for hundreds of millions of years. Legends remain of how it put to rest the clash between Kyogre and Groudon.

It flies forever through the ozone layer, consuming meteoroids for sustenance. The many meteoroids in its body provide the energy it needs to Mega Evolve.

RAYQUAZA → MEGA RAYQUAZA

MEGA RAYQUAZA

SKY HIGH POKÉMON
How to Say It: ray-KWAY-zuh
Imperial Height: 35'05"
Imperial Weight: 864.2 lbs.
Metric Height: 10.8 m
Metric Weight: 392.0 kg

Type: Dragon-Flying
Gender: Unknown
Abilities: Delta Stream
Weaknesses: Ice, Rock, Dragon, Fairy

#0378

With cold air that can reach temperatures as low as -328 degrees Fahrenheit, Regice instantly freezes any creature that approaches it.

This Pokémon's body is made of solid ice. It's said that Regice was born beneath thick ice in the ice age.

REGICE

ICEBERG POKÉMON
How to Say It: REDGE-ice
Imperial Height: 5'11"
Imperial Weight: 385.8 lbs.
Metric Height: 1.8 m
Metric Weight: 175.0 kg

Type: Ice
Gender: Unknown
Abilities: Clear Body
Weaknesses: Fire, Fighting, Rock, Steel

DOES NOT EVOLVE

#0895

An academic theory proposes that Regidrago's arms were once the head of an ancient dragon Pokémon. The theory remains unproven.

Its body is composed of crystallized dragon energy. Regidrago is said to have the powers of every dragon Pokémon.

REGIDRAGO

DRAGON ORB POKÉMON
How to Say It: REH-jee-dray-go
Imperial Height: 6'11"
Imperial Weight: 440.9 lbs.
Metric Height: 2.1 m
Metric Weight: 200.0 kg

Type: Dragon
Gender: Unknown
Abilities: Dragon's Maw
Weaknesses: Ice, Dragon, Fairy

DOES NOT EVOLVE

#0894

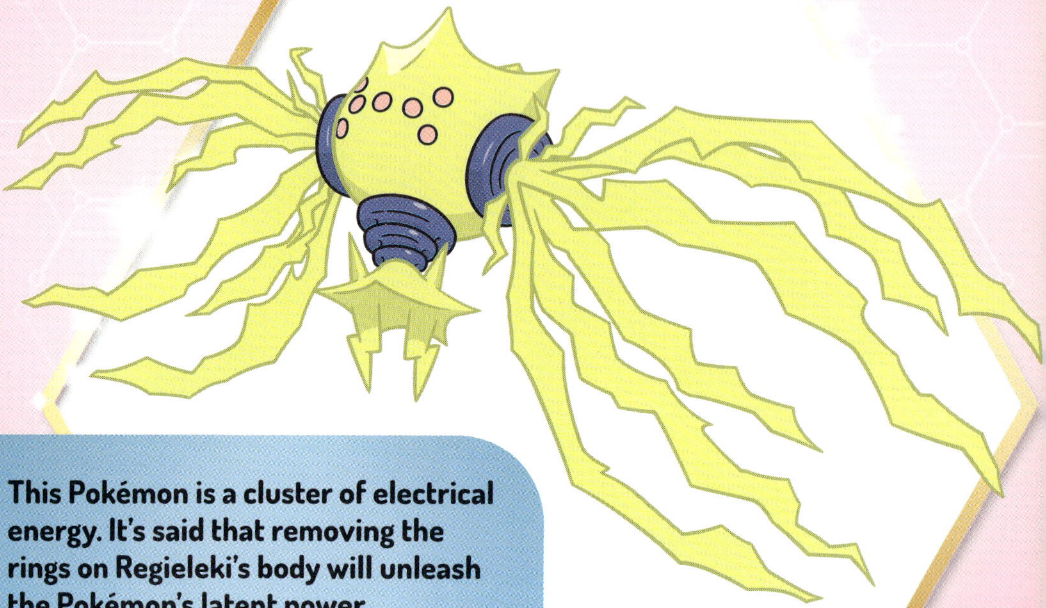

This Pokémon is a cluster of electrical energy. It's said that removing the rings on Regieleki's body will unleash the Pokémon's latent power.

Its entire body is made up of a single organ that generates electrical energy. Regieleki is capable of creating all Galar's electricity.

REGIELIKI

ELECTRON POKÉMON

How to Say It: REH-jee-uh-leh-kee

Imperial Height: 3'11"

Imperial Weight: 319.7 lbs.

Metric Height: 1.2 m

Metric Weight: 145.0 kg

Type: Electric

Gender: Unknown

Abilities: Transistor

Weaknesses: Ground

DOES NOT EVOLVE

#0486

It is said to have made Pokémon that look like itself from a special ice mountain, rocks, and magma.

There is an enduring legend that states this Pokémon towed continents with ropes.

REGIGIGAS

COLOSSAL POKÉMON
How to Say It: rej-jee-GIG-us
Imperial Height: 12'02"
Imperial Weight: 925.9 lbs.
Metric Height: 3.7 m
Metric Weight: 420.0 kg

Type: Normal
Gender: Unknown
Abilities: Slow Start
Weaknesses: Fighting

DOES NOT EVOLVE

#0377

Every bit of Regirock's body is made of stone. As parts of its body erode, this Pokémon sticks rocks to itself to repair what's been lost.

Cutting-edge technology was used to study the internals of this Pokémon's rock body, but nothing was found—not even a brain or a heart.

REGIROCK

ROCK PEAK POKÉMON
How to Say It: REDGE-ee-rock
Imperial Height: 5'07"
Imperial Weight: 507.1 lbs.
Metric Height: 1.7 m
Metric Weight: 230.0 kg

Type: Rock
Gender: Unknown
Abilities: Clear Body
Weaknesses: Water, Grass, Fighting, Ground, Steel

DOES NOT EVOLVE

#0379

Registeel's body is made of a strange material that is flexible enough to stretch and shrink but also more durable than any metal.

It's rumored that this Pokémon was born deep underground in the planet's mantle and that it emerged onto the surface 10,000 years ago.

REGISTEEL

IRON POKÉMON
How to Say It: REDGE-ee-steel
Imperial Height: 6'03"
Imperial Weight: 451.9 lbs.
Metric Height: 1.9 m
Metric Weight: 205.0 kg

Type: Steel
Gender: Unknown
Abilities: Clear Body
Weaknesses: Fire, Fighting, Ground

DOES NOT EVOLVE

#0643

This legendary Pokémon can scorch the world with fire. It helps those who want to build a world of truth.

When Reshiram's tail flares, the heat energy moves the atmosphere and changes the world's weather.

RESHIRAM

VAST WHITE POKÉMON
How to Say It: RESH-i-ram
Imperial Height: 10'06"
Imperial Weight: 727.5 lbs.
Metric Height: 3.2 m
Metric Weight: 330.0 kg

Type: Dragon-Fire
Gender: Unknown
Abilities: Turboblaze
Weaknesses: Ground, Rock, Dragon

DOES NOT EVOLVE

MYTHICAL POKÉMON

#0492

It can dissolve toxins in the air to instantly transform ruined land into a lush field of flowers.

The blooming of Gracidea flowers confers the power of flight upon it. Feelings of gratitude are the message it delivers.

LAND FORME

SHAYMIN

GRATITUDE POKÉMON
How to Say It: SHAY-min
Imperial Height: 0'08"
Imperial Weight: 4.6 lbs.
Metric Height: 0.2 m
Metric Weight: 2.1 kg

Type: Grass
Gender: Unknown
Abilities: Natural Cure
Weaknesses: Fire, Ice, Poison, Flying, Bug

DOES NOT EVOLVE

Turn the page to see another form of Shaymin!

#0492

It can dissolve toxins in the air to instantly transform ruined land into a lush field of flowers.

The blooming of Gracidea flowers confers the power of flight upon it. Feelings of gratitude are the message it delivers.

SKY FORME

SHAYMIN

GRATITUDE POKÉMON
How to Say It: SHAY-min
Imperial Height: 1'04"
Imperial Weight: 11.5 lbs.
Metric Height: 0.4 m
Metric Weight: 5.2 kg

Type: Grass-Flying
Gender: Unknown
Abilities: Serene Grace
Weaknesses: Fire, Ice, Poison, Flying, Rock

DOES NOT EVOLVE

#0773

A solid bond of trust between this Pokémon and its Trainer awakened the strength hidden within Silvally. It can change its type at will.

The final factor needed to release this Pokémon's true power was a strong bond with a Trainer it trusts.

TYPE: NULL

SILVALLY

SILVALLY

SYNTHETIC POKÉMON
How to Say It: sill-VAL-lie
Imperial Height: 7'07"
Imperial Weight: 221.6 lbs.
Metric Height: 2.3 m
Metric Weight: 100.5 kg

Type: Normal
Gender: Unknown
Abilities: RKS System
Weaknesses: Fighting

#0791

Sometimes the result of its opening an Ultra Wormhole is that energy and life-forms from other worlds are called here to this world.

In writings from the distant past, it's called by the name "the beast that devours the sun."

SOLGALEO

SUNNE POKÉMON
How to Say It: SOUL-gah-LAY-oh
Imperial Height: 11'02"
Imperial Weight: 507.1 lbs.
Metric Height: 3.4 m
Metric Weight: 230.0 kg

Type: Psychic-Steel
Gender: Unknown
Abilities: Full Metal Body
Weaknesses: Fire, Ground, Ghost, Dark

#0897

It probes its surroundings with all its senses save one—it doesn't use its sense of sight. Spectrier's kicks are said to separate soul from body.

As it dashes through the night, Spectrier absorbs the life-force of sleeping creatures. It craves silence and solitude.

SPECTRIER

SWIFT HORSE POKÉMON
How to Say It: SPEK-treer
Imperial Height: 6'07"
Imperial Weight: 98.1 lbs.
Metric Height: 2.0 m
Metric Weight: 44.5 kg

Type: Ghost
Gender: Unknown
Abilities: Grim Neigh
Weaknesses: Ghost, Dark

DOES NOT EVOLVE

#0245

Suicune embodies the compassion of a pure spring of water. It runs across the land with gracefulness. This Pokémon has the power to purify dirty water.

SUICUNE

AURORA POKÉMON
How to Say It: SWEE-koon
Imperial Height: 6'07"
Imperial Weight: 412.3 lbs.
Metric Height: 2.0 m
Metric Weight: 187.0 kg

Type: Water
Gender: Unknown
Abilities: Pressure
Weaknesses: Grass, Electric

DOES NOT EVOLVE

#0787

Although it's called a guardian deity, it's violent enough to crush anyone it sees as an enemy.

It makes ringing sounds with its tail to let others know where it is, avoiding unneeded conflicts. This guardian deity of Ula'ula controls plants.

TAPU BULU

LAND SPIRIT POKÉMON
How to Say It: TAH-poo BOO-loo
Imperial Height: 6'03"
Imperial Weight: 100.3 lbs.
Metric Height: 1.9 m
Metric Weight: 45.5 kg

Type: Grass-Fairy
Gender: Unknown
Abilities: Grassy Surge
Weaknesses: Fire, Ice, Poison, Fairy, Steel

DOES NOT EVOLVE

#0788

This guardian deity of Poni Island manipulates water. Because it lives deep within a thick fog, it came to be both feared and revered.

Although it's called a guardian deity, terrible calamities sometimes befall those who recklessly approach Tapu Fini.

TAPU FINI

LAND SPIRIT POKÉMON
How to Say It: TAH-poo FEE-nee
Imperial Height: 4'03"
Imperial Weight: 46.7 lbs.
Metric Height: 1.3 m
Metric Weight: 21.2 kg

Type: Water-Fairy
Gender: Unknown
Abilities: Misty Surge
Weaknesses: Grass, Electric, Poison

DOES NOT EVOLVE

#0785

Although it's called a guardian deity, if a person or Pokémon puts it in a bad mood, it will become a malevolent deity and attack.

The lightning-wielding guardian deity of Melemele, Tapu Koko is brimming with curiosity and appears before people from time to time.

TAPU KOKO

LAND SPIRIT POKÉMON
How to Say It: TAH-poo KO-ko
Imperial Height: 5'11"
Imperial Weight: 45.2 lbs.
Metric Height: 1.8 m
Metric Weight: 20.5 kg

Type: Electric-Fairy
Gender: Unknown
Abilities: Electric Surge
Weaknesses: Poison, Ground

DOES NOT EVOLVE

#0786

It heals the wounds of people and Pokémon by sprinkling them with its sparkling scales. This guardian deity is worshiped on Akala.

Although called a guardian deity, Tapu Lele is devoid of guilt about its cruel disposition and can be described as nature incarnate.

TAPU LELE

LAND SPIRIT POKÉMON
How to Say It: TAH-poo LEH-leh
Imperial Height: 3'11"
Imperial Weight: 41.0 lbs.
Metric Height: 1.2 m
Metric Weight: 18.6 kg

Type: Psychic-Fairy
Gender: Unknown
Abilities: Psychic Surge
Weaknesses: Poison, Ghost, Steel

DOES NOT EVOLVE

#1024

Terapagos protects itself using its power to transform energy into hard crystals. This Pokémon is the source of the Terastal phenomenon.

It's thought that this Pokémon lived in ancient Paldea until it got caught in seismic shifts and went extinct.

NORMAL FORM

TERAPAGOS

TERA POKÉMON
How to Say It: tehr-AH-puh-gohs
Imperial Height: 0'08"
Imperial Weight: 14.3 lbs.
Metric Height: 0.2 m
Metric Weight: 6.5 kg

Type: Normal
Gender: ♂ ♀
Abilities: Tera Shift
Weaknesses: Fighting

DOES NOT EVOLVE

Turn the page to see more forms of Terapagos!

#1024

Upon sensing danger, it prepares itself for battle by creating a sturdy shell of crystallized Terastal energy.

The shell is made of crystallized Terastal energy. When struck by a move, this shell absorbs the move's energy and transfers it to Terapagos.

TERASTALLIZED FORM

TERAPAGOS

TERA POKÉMON
How to Say It: ter-AH-puh-gohs
Imperial Height: 1'00"
Imperial Weight: 35.3 lbs.
Metric Height: 0.3 m
Metric Weight: 16.0 kg

Type: Normal
Gender: ♂ ♀
Abilities: Tera Shell
Weaknesses: Fighting

DOES NOT EVOLVE

#1024

In this form, Terapagos resembles the world as the ancients saw it, and its Terastal energy is abnormally amplified.

An old expedition journal describes the sight of this Pokémon buried in the depths of the earth as resembling a planet floating in space.

STELLAR FORM

TERAPAGOS

TERA POKÉMON
How to Say It: tehr-AH-puh-gohs
Imperial Height: 5'07"
Imperial Weight: 169.8 lbs.
Metric Height: 1.7 m
Metric Weight: 77.0 kg

Type: Normal
Gender: ♂ ♀
Abilities: Teraform Zero
Weaknesses: Fighting

DOES NOT EVOLVE

#0639

It has phenomenal power. It will mercilessly crush anyone or anything that bullies small Pokémon.

In Unovan legend, Terrakion battled against humans in an effort to protect other Pokémon.

TERRAKION

CAVERN POKÉMON
How to Say It: tur-RAK-ee-un
Imperial Height: 6'03"
Imperial Weight: 573.2 lbs.
Metric Height: 1.9 m
Metric Weight: 260.0 kg

Type: Rock-Fighting
Gender: Unknown
Abilities: Justified
Weaknesses: Water, Grass, Fighting, Ground, Psychic, Steel, Fairy

DOES NOT EVOLVE

#0642

The spikes on its tail discharge immense bolts of lightning. It flies around the Unova region firing off lightning bolts.

As it flies around, it shoots lightning all over the place and causes forest fires. It is therefore disliked.

INCARNATE FORME

THUNDURUS

BOLT STRIKE POKÉMON
How to Say It: THUN-duh-rus
Imperial Height: 4'11"
Imperial Weight: 134.5 lbs.
Metric Height: 1.5 m
Metric Weight: 61.0 kg

Type: Electric-Flying
Gender: ♂
Abilities: Prankster
Weaknesses: Ice, Rock

DOES NOT EVOLVE

Turn the page to see another form of Thundurus!

#0642

The spikes on its tail discharge immense bolts of lightning. It flies around the Unova region firing off lightning bolts.

As it flies around, it shoots lightning all over the place and causes forest fires. It is therefore disliked.

THERIAN FORME

THUNDURUS

BOLT STRIKE POKÉMON
How to Say It: THUN-duh-rus
Imperial Height: 9'10"
Imperial Weight: 134.5 lbs.
Metric Height: 3.0 m
Metric Weight: 61.0 kg

Type: Electric-Flying
Gender: ♂
Abilities: Volt Absorb
Weaknesses: Ice, Rock

DOES NOT EVOLVE

#1003

The fear poured into an ancient ritual vessel has clad itself in rocks and dirt to become a Pokémon.

It slowly brings its exceedingly heavy head down upon the ground, splitting the earth open with huge fissures that run over 160 feet deep.

TING-LU

RUINOUS POKÉMON
How to Say It: TIHNG-loo
Imperial Height: 8'10"
Metric Height: 2.7 m
Imperial Weight: 1,542.6 lbs.
Metric Weight: 699.7 kg

Type: Dark-Ground
Gender: Unknown
Abilities: Vessel of Ruin
Weaknesses: Fighting, Water, Ice, Fairy, Grass, Bug

DOES NOT EVOLVE

#0641

The lower half of its body is wrapped in a cloud of energy. It zooms through the sky at 200 mph.

Tornadus expels massive energy from its tail, causing severe storms. Its power is great enough to blow houses away.

INCARNATE FORME

TORNADUS

CYCLONE POKÉMON
How to Say It: tohr-NAY-dus
Imperial Height: 4'11"
Imperial Weight: 138.9 lbs.
Metric Height: 1.5 m
Metric Weight: 63.0 kg

Type: Flying
Gender: ♂
Abilities: Prankster
Weaknesses: Electric, Ice, Rock

DOES NOT EVOLVE

#0641

The lower half of its body is wrapped in a cloud of energy. It zooms through the sky at 200 mph.

Tornadus expels massive energy from its tail, causing severe storms. Its power is great enough to blow houses away.

THERIAN FORME

TORNADUS

CYCLONE POKÉMON
How to Say It: tohr-NAY-dus
Imperial Height: 4'07"
Imperial Weight: 138.9 lbs.
Metric Height: 1.4 m
Metric Weight: 63.0 kg

Type: Flying
Gender: ♂
Abilities: Regenerator
Weaknesses: Electric, Ice, Rock

DOES NOT EVOLVE

#0772

Rumor has it that the theft of top secret research notes led to a new instance of this Pokémon being created in the Galar region.

It was modeled after a mighty Pokémon of myth. The mask placed upon it limits its power in order to keep it under control.

TYPE: NULL

SYNTHETIC POKÉMON
How to Say It: TYPE NULL
Imperial Height: 6'03"
Imperial Weight: 265.7 lbs.
Metric Height: 1.9 m
Metric Weight: 120.5 kg

Type: Normal
Gender: Unknown
Abilities: Battle Armor
Weaknesses: Fighting

TYPE: NULL → SILVALLY

LEGENDARY POKÉMON

#0892

This form of Urshifu is a strong believer in the one-hit KO. Its strategy is to leap in close to foes and land a devastating blow with a hardened fist.

Inhabiting the mountains of a distant region, this Pokémon races across sheer cliffs, training its legs and refining its moves.

SINGLE STRIKE STYLE

URSHIFU

WUSHU POKÉMON

How to Say It: UR-shee-foo

Imperial Height: 6'03"

Imperial Weight: 231.5 lbs.

Metric Height: 1.9 m

Metric Weight: 105.0 kg

Type: Fighting-Dark

Gender: ♂ ♀

Abilities: Unseen Fist

Weaknesses: Fighting, Flying, Fairy

Turn the page to see more forms of Urshifu!

#0892

People call it the embodiment of rage. It's said that this Pokémon's terrifying expression and shout will rid the world of malevolence.

The energy released by this Pokémon's fists forms shock waves that can blow away Dynamax Pokémon in just one hit.

GIGANTAMAX URSHIFU SINGLE STRIKE STYLE

KUBFU → URSHIFU

WUSHU POKÉMON
How to Say It: UR-shee-foo
Imperial Height: 95'02"+
Imperial Weight: ?,???.? lbs.
Metric Height: 29.0+ m
Metric Weight: ???.? kg

Type: Fighting-Dark
Gender: ♂ ♀
Abilities: Unseen Fist
Weaknesses: Fighting, Flying, Fairy

#0892

It's believed that this Pokémon modeled its fighting style on the flow of a river—sometimes rapid, sometimes calm.

This form of Urshifu is a strong believer in defeating foes by raining many blows down on them. Its strikes are nonstop, flowing like a river.

KUBFU → URSHIFU

RAPID STRIKE STYLE

URSHIFU

WUSHU POKÉMON

How to Say It: UR-shee-foo

Imperial Height: 6'03"

Metric Height: 1.9 m

Imperial Weight: 231.5 lbs.

Metric Weight: 105.0 kg

Type: Fighting-Water

Gender: ♂ ♀

Abilities: Unseen Fist

Weaknesses: Grass, Electric, Flying, Psychic, Fairy

Turn the page to see another form of Urshifu!

#0892

As it waits for the right moment to unleash its Gigantamax power, this Pokémon maintains a perfect one-legged stance. It won't even twitch.

All it takes is a glare from this Pokémon to take the lives of those with evil in their hearts—or so they say.

GIGANTAMAX URSHIFU RAPID STRIKE STYLE

WUSHU POKÉMON
How to Say It: UR-shee-foo
Imperial Height: 84'04"+
Imperial Weight: ?,???.? lbs.
Metric Height: 26.0+ m
Metric Weight: ???.? kg

Type: Fighting-Water
Gender: ♂ ♀
Abilities: Unseen Fist
Weaknesses: Grass, Electric, Flying, Psychic, Fairy

#0480

Known as "The Being of Knowledge." It is said that it can wipe out the memory of those who see its eyes.

It is said that its emergence gave humans the intelligence to improve their quality of life.

UXIE

KNOWLEDGE POKÉMON
How to Say It: YOOK-zee
Imperial Height: 1'00"
Imperial Weight: 0.7 lbs.
Metric Height: 0.3 m
Metric Weight: 0.3 kg

Type: Psychic
Gender: Unknown
Abilities: Levitate
Weaknesses: Bug, Ghost, Dark

DOES NOT EVOLVE

#0494

This Pokémon brings victory. It is said that Trainers with Victini always win, regardless of the type of encounter.

When it shares the infinite energy it creates, that being's entire body will be overflowing with power.

VICTINI

VICTORY POKÉMON
How to Say It: vik-TEE-nee
Imperial Height: 1'04"
Imperial Weight: 8.8 lbs.
Metric Height: 0.4 m
Metric Weight: 4.0 kg

Type: Psychic-Fire
Gender: Unknown
Abilities: Victory Star
Weaknesses: Water, Ground, Rock, Ghost, Dark

DOES NOT EVOLVE

#0640

A legend tells of this Pokémon working together with Cobalion and Terrakion to protect the Pokémon of the Unova region.

It darts around opponents with a flurry of quick movements, slicing them up with its horns.

VIRIZION

GRASSLAND POKÉMON
How to Say It: vih-RYE-zee-un
Imperial Height: 6'07"
Imperial Weight: 440.9 lbs.
Metric Height: 2.0 m
Metric Weight: 200.0 kg

Type: Grass-Fighting
Gender: Unknown
Abilities: Justified
Weaknesses: Fire, Ice, Poison, Flying, Psychic, Fairy

DOES NOT EVOLVE

#0721

It lets out billows of steam and disappears into the dense fog. It's said to live in mountains where humans do not tread.

It expels its internal steam from the arms on its back. It has enough power to blow away a mountain.

VOLCANION

STEAM POKÉMON
How to Say It: vol-KAY-nee-un
Imperial Height: 5'07"
Imperial Weight: 429.9 lbs.
Metric Height: 1.7 m
Metric Weight: 195.0 kg

Type: Fire-Water
Gender: Unknown
Abilities: Water Absorb
Weaknesses: Electric, Ground, Rock

DOES NOT EVOLVE

#1001

The grudge of a person punished for writing the king's evil deeds upon wooden tablets has clad itself in dead leaves to become a Pokémon.

It drains the life force from vegetation, causing nearby forests to instantly wither and fields to turn barren.

WO-CHIEN

RUINOUS POKÉMON
How to Say It: WOH-chyehn
Imperial Height: 4'11"
Imperial Weight: 163.6 lbs.
Metric Height: 1.5 m
Metric Weight: 74.2 kg

Type: Dark-Grass
Gender: ♂ ♀
Abilities: Tablets of Ruin
Weaknesses: Fire, Flying, Fighting, Ice, Poison, Fairy, Bug

DOES NOT EVOLVE

#0716

Legends say it can share eternal life. It slept for a thousand years in the form of a tree before its revival.

When the horns on its head shine in seven colors, it is said to be sharing everlasting life.

XERNEAS

LIFE POKÉMON
How to Say It: ZURR-nee-us
Imperial Height: 9'10"
Imperial Weight: 474.0 lbs.
Metric Height: 3.0 m
Metric Weight: 215.0 kg

Type: Fairy
Gender: Unknown
Abilities: Fairy Aura
Weaknesses: Poison, Steel

DOES NOT EVOLVE

#0717

When this legendary Pokémon's wings and tail feathers spread wide and glow red, it absorbs the life force of living creatures.

When its life comes to an end, it absorbs the life energy of every living thing and turns into a cocoon once more.

YVELTAL

DESTRUCTION POKÉMON
How to Say It: ee-VELL-tall
Imperial Height: 19'00"
Imperial Weight: 447.5 lbs.
Metric Height: 5.8 m
Metric Weight: 203.0 kg

Type: Dark-Flying
Gender: Unknown
Abilities: Dark Aura
Weaknesses: Electric, Ice, Rock, Fairy

DOES NOT EVOLVE

#0888

Known as a legendary hero, this Pokémon absorbs metal particles, transforming them into a weapon it uses to battle.

This Pokémon has slumbered for many years. Some say it's Zamazenta's elder sister—others say the two Pokémon are rivals.

HERO OF MANY BATTLES

ZACIAN

WARRIOR POKÉMON
How to Say It: ZAH-shee-uhn
Imperial Height: 9'02"
Imperial Weight: 242.5 lbs.
Metric Height: 2.8 m
Metric Weight: 110.0 kg

Type: Fairy
Gender: Unknown
Abilities: Intrepid Sword
Weaknesses: Poison, Steel

DOES NOT EVOLVE

#0888

Now armed with a weapon it used in ancient times, this Pokémon needs only a single strike to fell even Gigantamax Pokémon.

Able to cut down anything with a single strike, it became known as the Fairy King's Sword, and it inspired awe in friend and foe alike.

CROWNED SWORD
ZACIAN

WARRIOR POKÉMON
How to Say It: ZAH-shee-uhn
Imperial Height: 9'02"
Imperial Weight: 782.6 lbs.
Metric Height: 2.8 m
Metric Weight: 355.0 kg

Type: Fairy-Steel
Gender: Unknown
Abilities: Intrepid Sword
Weaknesses: Fire, Ground

DOES NOT EVOLVE

#0889

In times past, it worked together with a king of the people to save the Galar region. It absorbs metal that it then uses in battle.

This Pokémon slept for aeons while in the form of a statue. It was asleep for so long, people forgot that it ever existed.

HERO OF MANY BATTLES

ZAMAZENTA

WARRIOR POKÉMON
How to Say It: ZAH-mah-ZEN-tuh
Imperial Height: 9'06"
Imperial Weight: 463.0 lbs.
Metric Height: 2.9 m
Metric Weight: 210.0 kg

Type: Fighting
Gender: Unknown
Abilities: Dauntless Shield
Weaknesses: Flying, Psychic, Fairy

DOES NOT EVOLVE

#0889

Its ability to deflect any attack led to it being known as the Fighting Master's Shield. It was feared and respected by all.

Now that it's equipped with its shield, it can shrug off impressive blows, including the attacks of Dynamax Pokémon.

CROWNED SHIELD

ZAMAZENTA

WARRIOR POKÉMON
How to Say It: ZAH-mah-ZEN-tuh
Imperial Height: 9'06"
Imperial Weight: 1,730.6 lbs.
Metric Height: 2.9 m
Metric Weight: 785.0 kg

Type: Fighting-Steel
Gender: Unknown
Abilities: Dauntless Shield
Weaknesses: Fire, Fighting, Ground

DOES NOT EVOLVE

#0145

This legendary Pokémon is said to live in thunderclouds. It freely controls lightning bolts.

ZAPDOS

ELECTRIC POKÉMON
How to Say It: ZAP-dose
Imperial Height: 5'03"
Imperial Weight: 116.0 lbs.
Metric Height: 1.6 m
Metric Weight: 52.6 kg

Type: Electric-Flying
Gender: Unknown
Abilities: Pressure
Weaknesses: Ice, Rock

DOES NOT EVOLVE

#0145

When its feathers rub together, they produce a crackling sound like the zapping of electricity. That's why this Pokémon is called Zapdos.

One kick from its powerful legs will pulverize a dump truck. Supposedly, this Pokémon runs through the mountains at over 180 mph.

GALARIAN ZAPDOS

STRONG LEGS POKÉMON
How to Say It: ZAP-dose
Imperial Height: 5'03"
Imperial Weight: 128.3 lbs.
Metric Height: 1.6 m
Metric Weight: 58.2 kg

Type: Fighting-Flying
Gender: Unknown
Abilities: Defiant
Weaknesses: Electric, Ice, Flying, Psychic, Fairy

DOES NOT EVOLVE

#0893

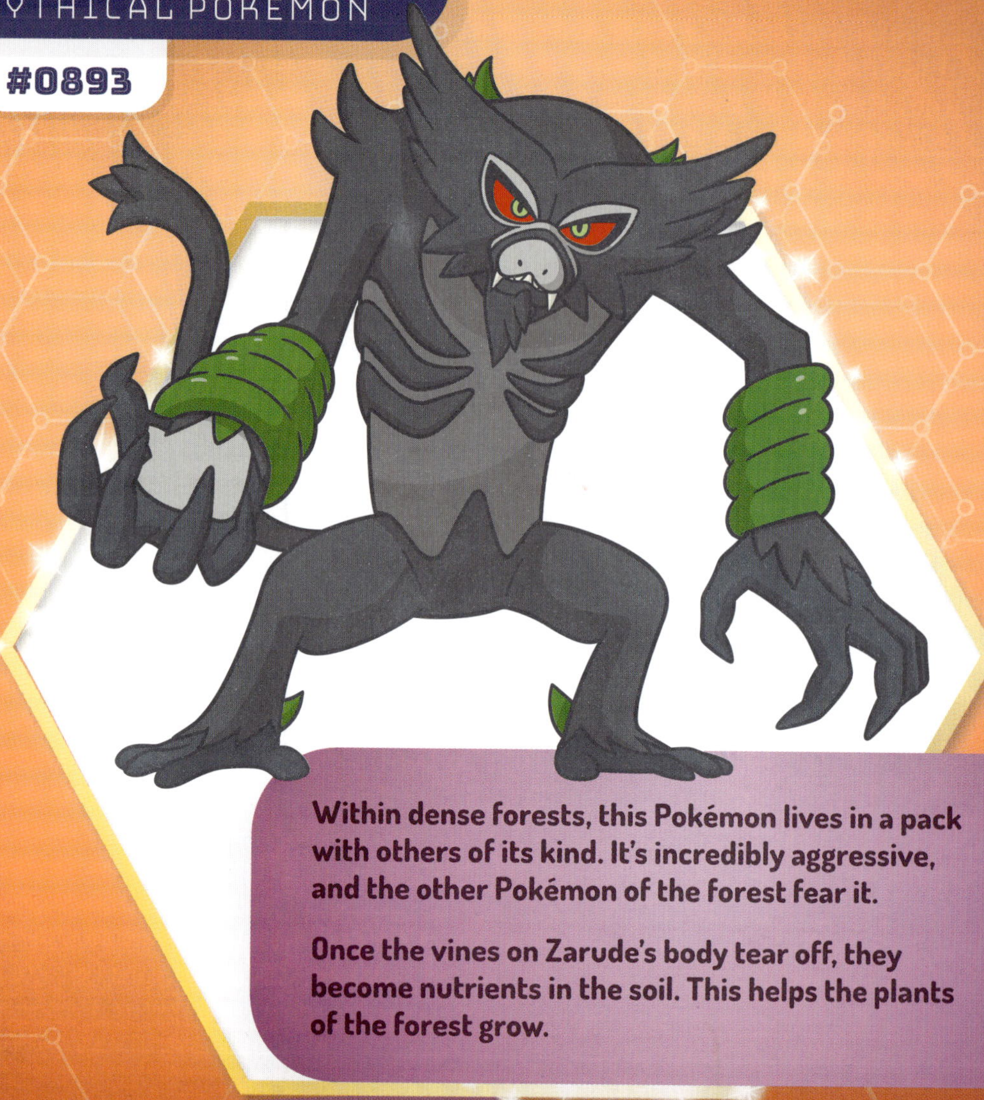

Within dense forests, this Pokémon lives in a pack with others of its kind. It's incredibly aggressive, and the other Pokémon of the forest fear it.

Once the vines on Zarude's body tear off, they become nutrients in the soil. This helps the plants of the forest grow.

ZARUDE

ROGUE MONKEY POKÉMON
How to Say It: zuh-ROOD
Imperial Height: 5'11"
Imperial Weight: 154.3 lbs.
Metric Height: 1.8 m
Metric Weight: 70.0 kg

Type: Dark-Grass
Gender: Unknown
Abilities: Leaf Guard
Weaknesses: Fire, Ice, Fighting, Poison, Flying, Bug, Fairy

DOES NOT EVOLVE

#0644

This legendary Pokémon can scorch the world with lightning. It assists those who want to build an ideal world.

Concealing itself in lightning clouds, it flies throughout the Unova region. It creates electricity in its tail.

ZEKROM

DEEP BLACK POKÉMON
How to Say It: ZECK-rahm
Imperial Height: 9'06"
Imperial Weight: 760.6 lbs.
Metric Height: 2.9 m
Metric Weight: 345.0 kg

Type: Dragon-Electric
Gender: Unknown
Abilities: Teravolt
Weaknesses: Ice, Ground, Dragon, Fairy

DOES NOT EVOLVE

#0807

It electrifies its claws and tears its opponents apart with them. Even if they dodge its attack, they'll be electrocuted by the flying sparks.

It approaches its enemies at the speed of lightning, then tears them limb from limb with its sharp claws.

ZERAORA

THUNDERCLAP POKÉMON
How to Say It: ZEH-rah-OH-rah
Imperial Height: 4'11"
Imperial Weight: 98.1 lbs.
Metric Height: 1.5 m
Metric Weight: 44.5 kg

Type: Electric
Gender: Unknown
Abilities: Volt Absorb
Weaknesses: Ground

DOES NOT EVOLVE

#0718

This is Zygarde's form when about half its pieces have been assembled. It plays the role of monitoring the ecosystem.

Some say it can change to an even more powerful form when battling those who threaten the ecosystem.

50% FORME

ZYGARDE

ORDER POKÉMON
How to Say It: ZY-gard
Imperial Height: 16'05"
Imperial Weight: 672.4 lbs.
Metric Height: 5.0 m
Metric Weight: 305.0 kg

Type: Dragon-Ground
Gender: Unknown
Abilities: Aura Break, Power Construct
Weaknesses: Ice, Dragon, Fairy

DOES NOT EVOLVE

Turn the page to see more forms of Zygarde!

#0718

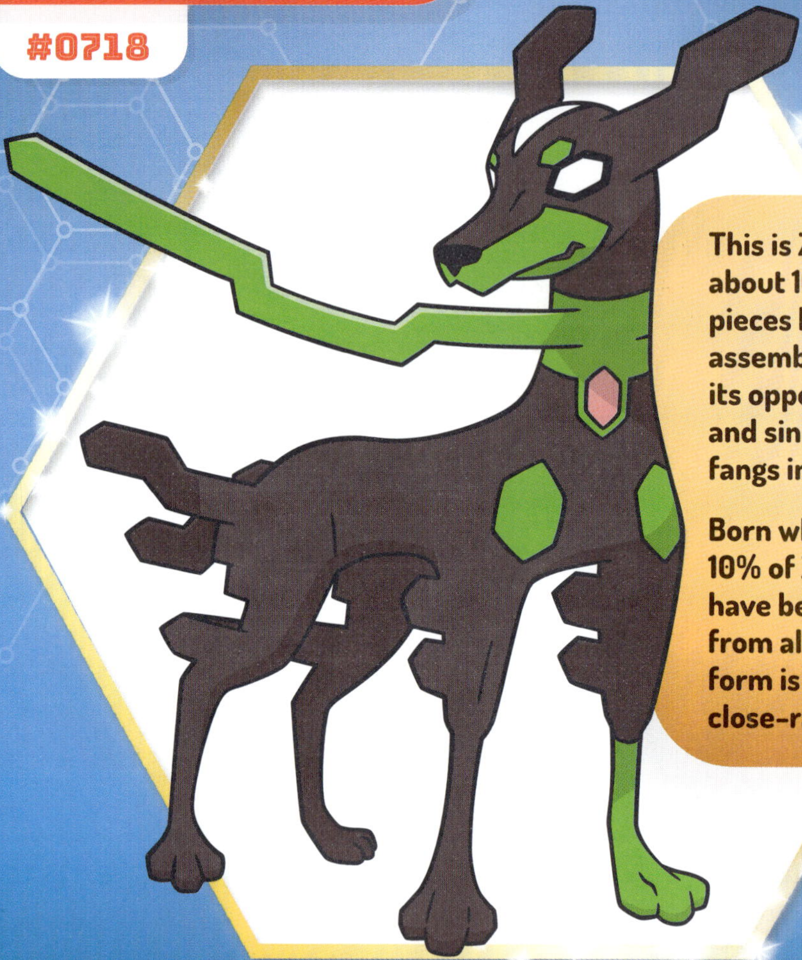

This is Zygarde when about 10% of its pieces have been assembled. It leaps at its opponent's chest and sinks its sharp fangs into them.

Born when around 10% of Zygarde's cells have been gathered from all over, this form is skilled in close-range combat.

10% FORME

ZYGARDE

ORDER POKÉMON
How to Say It: ZY-gard
Imperial Height: 3'11"
Imperial Weight: 73.9 lbs.
Metric Height: 1.2 m
Metric Weight: 33.5 kg

Type: Dragon-Ground
Gender: Unknown
Abilities: Aura Break, Power Construct
Weaknesses: Ice, Dragon, Fairy

DOES NOT EVOLVE

#0718

This is Zygarde's perfected form. From the orifice on its chest, it radiates high-powered energy that eliminates everything.

Born when all of Zygarde's cells have been gathered together, it uses force to neutralize those who harm the ecosystem.

COMPLETE FORME
ZYGARDE

ORDER POKÉMON
How to Say It: ZY-gard
Imperial Height: 14'09"
Imperial Weight: 1,344.8 lbs.
Metric Height: 4.5 m
Metric Weight: 610.0 kg

Type: Dragon-Ground
Gender: Unknown
Abilities: Power Construct
Weaknesses: Ice, Dragon, Fairy

DOES NOT EVOLVE

POKÉMON INDEX

Use this index to look up Legendary and Mythical Pokémon by National Pokédex Number!

National Pokédex Number	Name	Page Number(s)
144	Articuno	12, 13
145	Zapdos	148, 149
146	Moltres	83, 84
150	Mewtwo	78–81
151	Mew	76, 77
243	Raikou	103
244	Entei	34
245	Suicune	118
249	Lugia	65
250	Ho-Oh	46
251	Celebi	18
377	Regirock	110
378	Regice	106
379	Registeel	111
380	Latias	61, 62
381	Latios	63, 64
382	Kyogre	54, 55
383	Groudon	43, 44
384	Rayquaza	104, 105
385	Jirachi	49
386	Deoxys	26, 27
480	Uxie	137
481	Mesprit	75
482	Azelf	14
483	Dialga	28, 29
484	Palkia	99, 100
485	Heatran	45
486	Regigigas	109
487	Giratina	40, 41
488	Cresselia	24
489	Phione	102
490	Manaphy	68